DAILY BYTES

LESSONS FROM THE CORPORATE TRENCHES

ARUL SHANMUGAVELU

Made with ♥ on the Notion Press Platform
www.notionpress.com

Dedication

The learnings I gained from my colleagues & business associates throughout my career have been instrumental to writing this book. Each instance included in this book is based on my experiences with my colleagues and business associates, as well as my reflections on those experiences. It is with deep gratitude that I dedicate this book to all those who have contributed to my growth as a professional, including my junior colleagues, senior colleagues, peers, and business associates.

Thank you for making this journey possible.

Contents

Contents

Contents

Contents

Preface

What makes our life interesting is the change that it brings with it. If every day is a repeat of the previous day it will become very boring and we will lose interest in life. Due to this change, we encounter various situations in our professional careers and search for solutions to overcome the same.

Many books suggest various principles that help us in overcoming various challenges. However, applying those principles to our situations may be challenging as we need to distill the essence of the book and apply it to our situation.

In my earlier book on career development titled *French Fries*, I shared *15 golden ideas for powering your career growth*. These were very simple techniques with simple examples that you could relate to your daily situation. I received several appreciative emails from my esteemed readers expressing their delight over the examples that I had cited in that book. They expressed that they were able to relate to many of them and were able to find solutions to their problems.

Taking a cue from this, I wrote the book *Daily Bytes* with real-life anecdotes on various situations that a professional would come across in his or her professional career. There are 70 chapters covering topics from personality to business acumen. Each may not take more than two or three minutes to read.

You may choose to read them in any order. You can consider reading 1 title a day, just before going to sleep, and reflect the same on your experience. This would help in applying the learnings to your professional life.

Daily Bytes - Why This Title?

The name of my earlier book was French Fries, signaling that the subject matter will be easy to eat like French Fries, and it will also satiate hunger.

I wanted the title of this book also to be connected with food (similar to my earlier book) and at the same time reflect something intellectual. This book has several tiny to small chapters. Each chapter will take 2 to 3 minutes to read. It has an in-depth application value. I do not recommend reading this book at one stretch. I suggest that you keep the book on your bedside table. Read one topic a day. Reflect it so that the learning sinks. Daily bites will add bytes to your brain. Hence I titled this book *Daily Bytes*.

CHAPTER ONE

PERFECTION

Long ago, I visited our corporate head office to meet my boss. We were required to prepare a response letter to one of our overseas customers. After a short discussion, he asked me to make a draft of the letter for sending to the customer. He asked me to take the help of his secretary for typing the letter. (This was before laptop days). I took her help in preparing the letter. She typed it as I dictated. She took a printout and gave it to me. I went through the letter and there were a couple of mistakes which I corrected by pen. I was getting ready to meet my boss with the draft of the letter. The secretary told me "Please wait, I will make the corrections you have made and give you a new printout". I told her "Don't bother since there are only a couple of corrections and the boss is likely to make further corrections in the letter". She told me "Sir, I want to make sure that whatever goes out of my desk is perfect to the extent that I know of. Hence, please let me make those corrections and give you the corrected draft".

I am not sure whether it was a casual statement or not, but it lingers in my mind even after 20 years. I made it a point that whatever goes out of my desk is also perfect to the extent I am aware of. This can be as simple as a letter or as complicated as a tender.

We should own up to the activity that we are doing and make sure that it is perfect.

CHAPTER TWO

DO NOT TOLERATE MEDIOCRITY

In continuation to being perfect, it is also important not to tolerate mediocrity from our juniors and the people around us. As a customer, whether internal or external, you would be receiving products and services from others. This could be output from your junior colleague or the information received from your colleagues in the other departments. If it is short of perfection, please do not accept it. If we start accepting mediocrity within the organisation, then the mediocrity starts growing. If you become intolerant towards mediocrity, then it starts reducing. This is not only applicable to the official environment but also applicable to your personal life.

Let's assume that your junior colleague sent a mail to your customer, keeping you in copy. You find that the letter has a few mistakes. Please do not ignore it. Call your junior colleague and point out the improvements required.

In my professional life, I have learnt the most from difficult customers and from difficult bosses, who always demand nothing but the best. What you get is what you demand. Hence demand perfection from others and eliminate mediocrity.

CHAPTER THREE

GETTING TO KNOW PEOPLE AROUND YOU

It is good to know about the family of your colleagues. After all, we are social animals and our objective in life is not just to grow in our careers, but to co-exist peacefully. We spend most of our time in the office alongside our colleagues. It is only natural to get to know a little more about our colleagues. Of course, you need to appreciate the privacy that the other person wants to keep. I am not sure how this is taken in the Western world but in most parts of Eastern culture, getting to know the family strengthens the relationship and increases the bonding between the people. This creates a better working atmosphere in the office, where we spend most of our conscious time.

I used to receive guests (business associates) from Japan, the USA, Malaysia, Thailand, and some European countries. I made it a point to invite them home to have dinner with my family. My wife is a very good cook and she enjoyed cooking and was very happy to host them for dinner. The guests were also happy to come home, meet my family, have authentic Indian food, and understand our culture. During such visits, we got to know each other better. This helped me to build a good relationship with them.

I had a senior colleague by the name of N. Kameswaran, at L&T who was looking after Manufacturing when I was taking care of Marketing. We were good friends at the family level too. This made our job much easier and we were able to address the needs of the customer more easily. I never enjoyed such comfort with any other manufacturing people with whom I worked later. It helped us to provide better service to our customers.

After reaching the position of the Managing Director of the company, I made it a point to meet every individual employee on a one-on-one basis to get to know them better. In this meeting, it was agreed that no official matters will be discussed. This helps me to build a rapport with my team. In addition, it helps to learn something new from them. As in any other company, the employees in our company are also from different backgrounds, different age groups, etc. Talking to them helped me to understand the world better.

CHAPTER FOUR

READING HABIT

Reading books is a great way to enhance your knowledge. I do not know whether all people who read books are successful in their careers, but what I know is that successful people read books regularly.

It is also true that reading books on new subjects activates your brain cells and makes them brisker. Hence, I strongly recommend you to read books of your interest that will help you grow in your career and improve your personality.

There are plenty of books available in the market which could help in increasing your knowledge. At this juncture, I would like to caution you not to fall prey to the pride of knowledge which inhibits the application of knowledge. I have known people who boost the knowledge they have gained but have miserably failed to grow in their careers as they did not apply their learning.

Knowing things is of no use unless you can do something with them. For eg. reading a book on cooking is useless unless you apply the knowledge by making a few fine dishes. Please make it a habit to put into practice some of the points that you have learnt from a book. I strongly recommend that you should not touch the next book unless you have put into practice a few of the learnings from the book that you just finished reading.

Many people ask me, “What is the number of books a person should read to be successful?”. If you ask Google, it would say "CEOs read 60 books a year". I am not sure whether this is true or practical. What is important is how much of the learnings you can put into practice.

The selection of a book of your interest is very important. Nowadays there are several reviews available on the internet, by many people including several celebrities. You could identify some of them and follow their reviews. One of the most popular ones is by Bill Gates (gatesnotes.com)

There are many such reviews that I urge you to go through for selecting the book of your choice.

CHAPTER FIVE

NEVER FAIL TO EXPRESS YOUR OPINION

When you attend a meeting, you may be faced with a dilemma of whether you should express your opinion or not, especially when your boss is chairing the meeting.

In a typical meeting with your boss, you might be agreeing to his/her proposal because you felt that he/ she is the right person to decide or maybe because you feel that boss will not listen to you, even if you raise your views.

Kindly note that a boss is not a superhuman who has solutions to every problem. The boss also struggles with many options before taking a decision. If a boss has a bunch of people who just accept or repeat whatever he or she says, then the decision-making process suffers. Professional managers love to receive ideas and thoughts that are different from their thoughts.

I strongly recommend that you express your opinions forthright to your colleagues and your boss, however divergent it may be, provided there is a strong reason for your saying so. Ensure that you logically convey your opinion by explaining the background properly. Do not worry whether your boss accepts your idea or not. What is important is the process of decision-making. If there are no divergent views discussed in the meeting, then the quality of the decision suffers. At the same time, you should also have the maturity of accepting the final decision of the team even if they are different from yours.

To achieve success, an organization must encourage diverse opinions and open communication in meetings. However, once the meeting concludes, it's essential that all team members set aside any differences and come together as a unified team.

In organizations that suffer from mediocracy, differences are is never raised in the meetings. It gives the impression that all agree with the decision. But when the members go out of the room, none of them own up to the decision and as a result, their commitment to action suffers.

I always look forward to discussing and reflecting on my thoughts with a person who normally disagrees with my thoughts rather than with people who generally agree with my thoughts.

Professional managers look for people who are forthright in their expressions and not people who say "yes" to the boss all the time.

CHAPTER SIX

DELEGATION

Delegation of work is one of the important and difficult skills that one should learn while growing in his or her career.

When a person starts his career, his performance depends on his skill and capacity. As the person starts to grow in the hierarchy, he is expected to get the work done by other people and his performance depends on the performance of others. Some people fail at this point as they fail to delegate. This not only affects the individual but also the company.

As you grow in your career, you are expected to contribute more. The contribution can increase only if you synergise the activities of others with yours.

Some people fail to delegate their work to their subordinates because they fear that the subordinate may not perform the job as well as they want it to be done. Some feel insecure that the sub-ordinate may do a better job and challenge them. This insecurity can be overcome by upskilling/upgrading your knowledge and skill continuously.

Effective delegation can be achieved by identifying the right person to whom the job can be delegated and training him to perform that job properly. Based on the criticality of the activity, you need to build checkpoints to ensure that the output is in line with your expectation. Unless you learn this skill, you will get stuck in your current position, because you become indispensable in that position.

Delegation is a mandatory skill that should be developed to ensure one's growth.

CHAPTER SEVEN

The Art of Delegation

Delegation is an art. It needs to be learnt and practised. However, when we are faced with a situation wherein we are required to delegate some of our work, we may face the following situations.

1. Your junior to whom you are delegating your work may be a fresher or new to this job and hence does not know how to do it. At this time you may be faced with a dilemma of whether to spend time teaching the junior or doing the job yourselves, Doing it yourselves may consume a fraction of the time that you are required to spend on teaching. If you do not spend time teaching your junior now, you are never going to delegate your job. You might have heard the following story. A woodcutter was very busy cutting a tree with his saw. After some time, the saw became blunt and was not cutting efficiently. A person who was watching this told him that the saw has become blunt and it needs to be sharpened. The woodcutter replied, "I am very busy cutting the wood and I don't have time to sharpen the

saw". Unfortunately, some of us do not realize that the time we spend teaching our juniors will help us save time in the future.

2. When you delegate the job to your junior colleague he may do it in a different method than what you are used to. This may make you uncomfortable. Please understand that your process may not be the only correct process. Please check the method followed by your junior for its robustness and accuracy. If you are satisfied, then you need not worry. If not, please explain your concern and correct the method of your junior.
3. Since the job is critical, you may want to do the job yourself rather than give it to your junior. Kindly recall how your boss trusted you when you were a junior. Is it because you were smarter compared to your current junior? Hmm, the possibilities are Yes and No. Probably your boss had a method of ensuring that your output is acceptable. Similarly, you need to develop certain checkpoints to verify that the output is correct.
4. If you still find that your subordinate is not up to the mark you may explore a method of deskilling the process through automation. In the current era of software-driven processes, many areas can be deskilled so that they can be performed by lesser competent people.
5. You may do that job in an extremely proficient way, which may be due to the expertise you have gained over several years. Is it fair to expect the same from a person who is yet to learn the skill? Please check whether your expectation of the output from your junior is fair.

CHAPTER EIGHT

LEARN & SHARE KNOWLEDGE

Some people consider knowledge as power and refuse to share it with others. Knowledge is no more power. In this internet world, knowledge can be easily accessed. It will benefit you more when you share it with others. When you share it with your younger colleagues, the work they do improves, and the performance of your department improves. This also helps you to groom them for your position and thus enabling you to move up the ladder. At times, people get stuck at one level (without growth) because they have not groomed a person for their position.

When you share your knowledge with your colleagues, it strengthens your understanding of the subject and makes you an expert on the subject. The natural fear amongst most of us is that when we share with our colleague, it will make him equivalent to us and he will compete with us. You are right, sharing with a colleague will help him to upgrade. This will put pressure on you to learn further and be ahead of him. Even if you do not teach him, he will learn it anyway, maybe a bit later, and you may not be even aware that he has learnt it and probably he learnt it better than you.

After I completed my engineering degree in 1984, I was lucky to get a campus placement, which was very rare in those days. The placement was with HCL Limited, in their factory at Dehradun. At that time, HCL was making photocopiers in that facility, with the help of technology from Toshiba, Japan. They had a nice little machine shop where I was posted. I was a fresher from college and did not have practical knowledge about machines. Since I was a graduate engineer, I was at a higher grade and had a couple of experienced diploma engineers reporting to me. One of them (Hari Harinath) took lots of pain to educate me on the machines and their criticalities. I asked him, "Are you not scared that if you teach me, I will learn the job quickly, and I will start questioning you?" Hari replied, "Arul, even if I don't teach you, you will learn it anyway. So, I am not scared to teach you. Moreover when I teach others, I get better clarity on the subject". He winked and added, "Because I taught you something, I am sure you will not hesitate to teach me in areas where you are better than me".

Learning and sharing is a continuous process that should not stop till our last breath.

CHAPTER NINE

FOLLOW YOUR PASSION

Career growth in the corporate world is not the only destination that everyone should strive for. It depends on your interest. I would like to share with you the following true story of a passionate man who choose a career to help underprivileged people instead of a corporate career.

Mr. Ramesh completed his B.Sc in Mathematics and was preparing for his Chartered Account exams. He is from a very poor family. A girl distantly related to him asked his help to do her Higher Secondary (+2). She had secured good marks in thc 10th standard. Since her family is also very poor, they were not ready to send her for further studies. Ramesh somehow helped her to join the 11th standard and also told her that if she secured good marks in the 12th standard he would help her to join medicine and make her a doctor, which was her dream. He told this casually, to encourage her to study well. He had no idea whether and how he can help her. She secured very high marks in the 12th standard which made it easy for her to get a medical seat. She asked Ramesh to help, as promised earlier!

Ramesh did not even have a job at that time. But he felt that he should help this girl pursue her studies. He went around asking many people to help her to study. Due to his genuine approach and sheer persuasion, he managed to get a sponsor for that girl to pursue her education. This action gave enormous satisfaction to Ramesh and he decided to dedicate his life to helping people to study and thus founded an institution called Mugavari Foundation.

Through this foundation, over 500 students have benefitted (as of 2022). Out of this, over 100 students are medical students. His job does not end with just seeking donations from people and channelizing them to help the poor people. He formed a virtual community of these students who regularly interact with one another which helps them to improve their personalities.

When a person follows his/ her dreams strongly the avenues open on their own. Believing strongly in your dream increases the likelihood of realizing it.

The contribution that Mr. Ramesh is making to society is phenomenal. The world survives due to the selfless contribution of such people. To serve society, age or wealth or position are not the barriers. It is the mind. If you are determined you will certainly find a way, like Mr. Ramesh.

CHAPTER TEN

EMOTIONAL BANK ACCOUNT

Closing Balance: **INR 6,287.69**

Date	Narration	Cheque/Ref. No.	Value Date	Withdrawal	Deposit	Closing Balance
01 Oct 2021	Credit Interest Capitalised		30 Sep 2021		112.00	6,287.69
26 Sep 2021	IB FUNDS TRANSFER DR-00101000013791 -S ARUL	IB26165856569507	26 Sep 2021	15,000.00		6,175.69
02 Sep 2021	ACH C- MARUTI SUZUKI INDIA-0000000000000	007079200245	02 Sep 2021		2,250.00	21,175.69
01 Sep 2021	ACH C- ICICI BANK LTD-IB29163479	004929266628	01 Sep 2021		600.00	18,925.69

A typical financial Bank Account

An interpersonal relationship is one of the most important skills that a person should develop to lead a peaceful and successful life, both personally and professionally. Amongst many concepts being taught on managing relationships, I consider Emotional Bank Account (EBA) to be the most effective.

In the book "The 7 Habits of Highly Effective People" the author Stephen R. Covey explains this concept of EBA.

Though I read this book 25 years ago, the EBA is etched in my mind very strongly.

We are all aware of how our bank account operates. We deposit money in our account and the bank allows us to withdraw our money. If there is a NIL balance in our account, we cannot withdraw. EBA also works on a similar principle.

When person A makes a positive impact on person B by comforting him/ her during despair or teaching him/her something important or helping in some manner, person A deposits into the EBA he has with person B. In a professional environment, assisting a colleague in doing his or her work or delighting an internal customer, or honouring a commitment, makes a deposit in the EBA with the person who receives the service. The amount of the deposit depends on the activity. A small help deposits a small amount and a big help deposits a larger amount into the EBA.

When there is an argument or a situation where your action hurts the other person, you make a withdrawal from your EBA with the other person. If you make more withdrawals than your deposit, naturally your account will run into negative (overdraft). If you have enough credit in the EBA, an unintentional hurt by you may not affect your relationship, since there is a balance in the account, even after the withdrawal caused by your hurt. Sometimes people overdraw from this EBA and end up as a debtor (emotionally) to the other person. In such as case, any interaction between these 2 persons ends up in arguments, even on small issues.

Like in the bank, where their clients are allowed to overdraw based on their relationship or the collateral securities that they may have, in the human relationship also, this overdrawing facility is available. Typically, this over-withdrawal happens between Parents and Children and between spouses, because of the love, affection, or care one person has for the other. Sometimes, without our knowledge, we stretch it too far resulting in a breakup of the relationship.

At any given opportunity please consider depositing into the EBA with the other person, who matters to you in your personal & professional life. This will make the interpersonal relationship more peaceful, successful, and enjoyable.

CHAPTER ELEVEN

PREPARING THE SOIL

I would like to narrate an incident that happened in my professional career, which could have ended up as a standoff between me (our company) and the customer, had I not handled it properly.

About a decade ago, the company where I worked, had supplied several machines to one of its customers in the United States (US). The headquarters (HQ) of this customer was in Europe and our supplies were to its plant in the US. All technical and commercial discussions took place in the HQ in Europe. Based on this we supplied our machines to the end-user in the US. Unfortunately, there was a major shortcoming in the machine due to a communication gap between the HQ in Europe, the end-user in the US, and we in India. To resolve this shortcoming in the machine, we had several meetings through teleconferences amongst all three parties. Each of us was sticking to our point and hence we were not reaching an agreement. The end-user in the US was insisting on a replacement of all the machines that were supplied by us. This would be a financial and reputational disaster, although we can not be fully blamed for it. Moreover, the replacement of the machines was not warranted as it required only an additional module (assembly) to meet the requirements of the end user. Despite several rounds of discussions, we were not heading anywhere. Mainly because none of us was willing to give in. Probably we all felt that "giving in" will be considered a weakness and acceptance of the mistake.

I and my colleague discussed how to resolve this. A final teleconference was scheduled for the next day. There was enormous pressure on us. If we don't arrive at a solution it was going to be a major setback for us in the US market. We decided that instead of arguing in the meeting where three parties were present, we felt that we should have a discussion with one of the parties separately and see whether a solution can be reached. If this is successful, we should find a way to put this across in the formal meeting.

I had a telephone discussion with the person in the HQ, with whom we dealt during the order finalization. Both of us discussed the situation and the possible ramifications of not reaching a conclusion. I proposed that we would supply the additional module (sub-assy) at a discounted price and also depute our engineer for fixing the same. I requested his acceptance. Since he was also interested in resolving the impasse, he agreed to the same.

I suggested to him that he should make the above demand on us in the meeting scheduled the next day and we would accept the same. I also explained to him why I am asking him to make this demand on us. I told him that if we make this proposal from our side, both parties will hesitate to accept due to the risk of being seen as weak in front of the supplier. He agreed to my proposal.

In the meeting held on the next day, as planned the person from the HQ made the above proposal and we accepted the proposal. This put an end to the impasse, to the satisfaction of all. This resulted in a stronger relationship between the companies and till today this customer is a major customer of the company.

In many situations, whether personal or professional, it may not be possible for us to resolve issues in a formal discussion. It is necessary to prepare the participants before the meeting for a possible solution. It is like preparing the soil before the seeds are sowed so that it sprouts well.

CHAPTER TWELVE

The Balancing Act

I had a senior colleague who was taking care of one of the product divisions of our company. Generally, I used to spend about an hour beyond office hours to contact some of our customers in different time zones. I used to observe that this senior colleague was staying even after I left the office. What was very surprising to me was that I never saw him doing any work beyond office hours but still, he used to sit in the office. He was a very nice and friendly person.

I asked him one day "Sir, why don't you go home, it's already late. I don't see you busy with any work. Moreover, all your team members have left the office". He replied, "Arul, you are right, I don't have any work now, however, I do not know what to do if I go home now". I asked him, "Is your family not in town?". He replied, "They are very much in town. I am used to going home very late for many years and hardly had any time to have meaningful discussions with them in the past. They have learnt to live with my absence and if I now go early now, it will be an intrusion into their privacy. I also feel very odd because I do not know how to engage my family in a casual conversation". I was shocked to hear this.

Another colleague of mine who worked in Mumbai used to work for more than 12 hours in the factory every day. He was doing this for many years. He had no idea what his children were doing. By the time he realised he had not spent quality time with his family, the children got married and started their life. He hardly has any contact with them now.

I am not sure whether the above sounds familiar or unbelievable to you. Please be assured that these are real incidents.

The point that I am trying to bring to your attention is that our life is not only about our profession. There are many things beyond our profession. Our family is important in our life and career growth cannot be achieved by spoiling our relationship with family members. The growth in the professional career brings with it higher income, more responsibilities, more authority, etc. All these could have a mesmerising effect on us and make us forget other priorities in life. My humble request to you is to balance the priorities between your personal and professional life.

CHAPTER THIRTEEN

REFLECTING ON EBA

Kindly read Chapter 10 on Emotional Bank Account before reading this Chapter.

When we show our kindness to another person, we make a deposit in our emotional bank account (EBA) with them. Sometimes the receiving party may take us for granted. This is probably one of the reasons why peers in an organization do not build emotional bank accounts with one another. It may also be due to the competitiveness between the peers, in their career growth.

Genuine EBA activities can be built through regular functional activities, which when done in a good manner can make a deposit in the EBA.

When you share important information, which will be useful for the other person professionally, you build the EBA.

When the engineering team leader delivers a drawing to the manufacturing team and takes pain to explain to the manufacturing team the nuances involved in the manufacturing of a component, he builds the EBA.

When a person in a purchase function helps the manufacturing team or the engineering team to tide over a difficult situation, with the help of their vendor base, without making a big fuss, he builds the EBA. (Doing a help and publicizing it does more harm than good)

Such genuine activities do not lower the stature of the person who's doing this activity.

In the case of Boss and Sub-ordinate, it comes naturally because such an act does not change the relationship that they currently hold as a boss or a subordinate.

When it comes to a family situation, where the positions are clearly defined such as father, mother, husband, wife, and children, I feel there should be no hesitation in depositing in the EBA. It is not going to change any of our positions in the relationship.

If you have not been depositing in the EBA of a family member you may have some hesitation in starting it suddenly. This is because we seldom like to change our masks. I guess it does not matter since this change can only help in having an enjoyable relationship. I remember what my father told me when I got (arranged) married. (As you may know, in an arranged marriage you do not know to what kind of a person you are getting married.) My dad said, "Arul, no matter whether your wife likes you or not, shower love on her without expecting anything in return." He said, "Trust me, even if she does not like you initially, your actions will make her reciprocate with more love sooner than later". I followed it and I did not have to wait longer.

CHAPTER FOURTEEN

APOLOGISE WHEN YOU HURT SOMEONE

Life is about co-existence in diversity. In day-to-day life, we are required to interact with many people, known and unknown.

During our regular interactions, it is quite possible that we hurt people through our words and actions. Sometimes we feel that our irate reaction was unwarranted for the situation or we made an incorrect statement that hurt someone in the group. As soon as we realise it, we must apologize to the person for our actions and words. This is not a strategy, but it is only being human with our fellow citizens of the world. Seeking an apology is never a weakness of a personality, I consider that to be the strength of a personality. However, never offer an apology if you are not convinced that you were wrong. Also, do not offer an apology insincerely. An insincere apology will do more harm than good.

In case you have hurt someone in public it is only fair to offer an apology also in public. It will be unfair to hurt someone in public and apologise in private.

If you have watched the movie Zindagi Na Milegi Dobara, you may remember that Hrithik Roshan, Abhay Deol, and Farhan Akhtar were friends. Hrithik would be angry with Farhan since Farhan fell in love with Hrithik Roshan's girlfriend and she would leave Hrithik for Farhan. This would have hurt Hrithik Roshan, a lot (naturally). Later she dumps Farhan also. 4 years later they would travel to Europe to celebrate the engagement of Abhay. During this trip, Hrithik and Farhan will have an altercation wherein Hrithik will cite what Farhan did to him. Farhan will say, "I have said sorry many times for this and how many more times should I say sorry for this". Hrithik will say, "Till you say it from the heart". This nicely explains that until the sorry comes from the heart, it is meaningless.

It is often said that offering an apology is human and accepting an apology is divine. Sometimes, we will not be in a position to forgive someone, because the person has done such harm that we are unable to forget. It is said that carrying remorse does a lot of harm to our health and forgiving gives great relief to the person and allows him or her to move forward. If you feel that there is certain hurt in you that you can not forgive someone for the crime done, please watch the video "I Survived the Holocaust Twin Experiments"

In this video, you will see a victim of a second world war holocaust (Nazi camp) Ms. Eva Moses Kor writing a letter of amnesty (forgiveness) to all the people involved in this nasty Holocaust. If she can forgive the world's worst crime on humankind, I do not think we have any reason not to forgive a person.

Offer an apology, grant amnesty and free yourself of hard feelings.

CHAPTER FIFTEEN

YOUR FUTURE IS NOT IN THE JOB YOU HOLD, IT IS IN WHAT YOU DO WITH THE JOB

I recently read the following story in the book Mentoring by John C Maxwell. It was very interesting and hence I thought I could share it with others as well. The author refers to an article he read in a magazine a few decades ago titled "Sel, not Spel". I'm sure you do not understand what this means. You will surely understand it at the end of the story.

A salesman wrote his first sales report to the Head Office, after working in his territory for the first week. It shocked the Sales Manager as he realized that he hired someone who does not even know how to write a correct English sentence. Here is what the report read, "I went and seen this outfit ain't never bot nothin from us befour and I sole em a good order. Now I am movin on to Nu Yourk."

The manager was in a panic but before he could get hold of the salesman to fire him, he received the second report it said, "I done been here fer too days and sole them half a million"

Then the manager was confused he could not keep an illiterate salesman, but he could not fire a salesman who had outsold everyone else in the sales force in his second week of employment. So, he did what every good middle manager does: he dumped the problem in the lap of the company's President.

The next morning everyone in the sales department was amazed to see the salesman's two letters on the bulletin board along with the following memo from the President: "We bin spendin weigh two much time tryin to spel in stead of tryin to sel. Let's all try to get our sails up. Reed these too letters from hour best salsman. He is doin a great job and all you shud go out and do like he done."

The author ends by citing Doctor George W crane, "There is no future in any job, the future lies in the person who holds the job."

I experienced this in my career. We had salesmen to market our product in all four regions East, West, North, and South of India. All our salesmen were engineers from good colleges carefully selected, except a person in the Eastern region. He had not gone to college but somehow managed to be in a sales job for many years. I was a fresher in marketing when I met him 30 years ago. He took me to his customers in the eastern region. The amount of rapport he enjoyed with his customers at all levels starting from the clerk to the President was amazing. To be honest, I can not match his skill of relationship building. Until he retired, the company did not even think of replacing him with a qualified person. This proves the point, "There is no future in any job, the future lies in the person who holds the job."

Your future is not in the job you hold, it is in what you do with the job

CHAPTER SIXTEEN

The Success Mechanism Is A Normally Closed Valve

Everyone has an equal amount of time, but some people use it more efficiently and effectively than others. What makes a person successful or not, depends on to what extent he utilizes his potential in the given time. (I would like to clarify that "success" means different things to different people. For someone, earning money may be a success, for another person, it may be power & position, for a third person it may be having a happy family, for yet another person it may be serving society.)

While everyone wants to succeed in life why do only a few make it?

I would like to explain with a simple example of a pipeline.

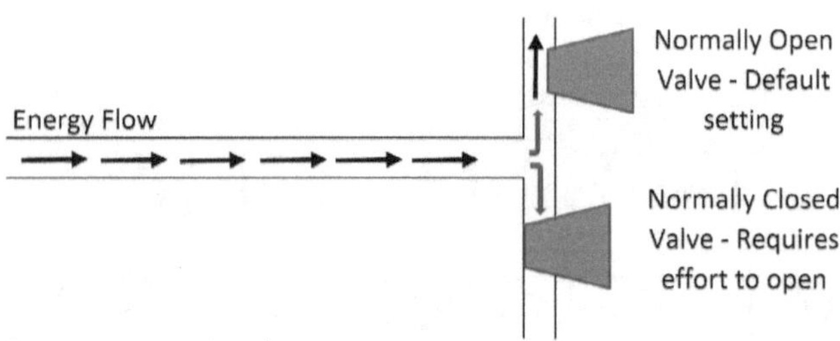

Energy Flow Diagram

Please refer to the pipeline shown above. It has 2 outlets, one fitted with a valve which is always open and another fitted with a valve which is always closed. The energy that we have is like the water that could flow through this pipeline. It will go out through the outlet where the valve is kept open. This is the default setting for most of us. For example, most people may spend time watching TV, social media, online games, browsing, binge-watching, chatting, etc. For all these activities you need not put any special effort.

But if you need to achieve something / succeed, you need to channel your energy through the closed valve (the "normally closed valve").

Opening this valve needs effort and commitment. Successful people put effort to close the "Normally Open" valve and open the "Normally Closed" valve. By doing this they channel their time and energy to achieve their goal, which was being wasted doing useless activities. Please identify the normally closed valve that is stopping you from achieving success and open it to channel your energy.

Let me cite an example of how we can open the valve to success. For example, let us assume you would like to go jogging every day in the morning. It is one of the most difficult things for many of us. In the morning when you get up the failure mechanism works and does not allow you to go jogging, which is your goal. We need to find a way to open the success valve so that you can channel your efforts to go jogging. One of the ways is to find a companion for doing this. Find a person who jogs daily, please tell him you will join from tomorrow. When you know your friend will be waiting for you at 6:00 AM to go jogging, it forces you to get up and go.

Similarly, let us imagine that you would like to qualify yourself further by attending an evening college. The thought of committing every evening to go to college may cause great stress. In such a case you could find a like-minded person who would like to further his studies and both of you could jointly do this activity. This would reduce the stress and help you to open the success valve.

Another way is to visualize the result that you will get by doing the activity, like a healthy body, better knowledge, chatting with a friend, etc. This can help you to open your valve for success. Once you get used to opening this valve often, the valve could become a normally open valve and channel your energy towards achieving your goal.

Find your valve and open it, you will find a new world.

CHAPTER SEVENTEEN

YOUR SUCCESS IN YOUR HANDS

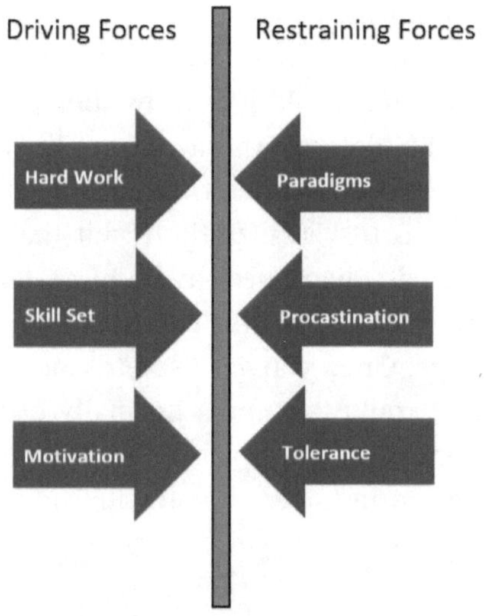

Force Field Diagram

Progress in our life is the result of driving forces and restraining forces. If the driving force is greater than the restraining forces then we progress in our life. If the restraining force is greater than the driving force, then we deteriorate in our position. For many of us, we reach equilibrium and we stagnate in that position or we move at a very marginal speed.

The driving force in our life is a combination of many factors such as our educational qualification, our skill sets, our ability to do hard work / smart work, the level of motivation that we have, support from family & friends, our network, etc. All these act as a thrust for growing our career.

On the other hand, the restraining forces are; our paradigms in life, lack of qualification, tolerance towards our current situation (dissatisfaction), etc.

Dissatisfaction with the current situation is one of the major elements which can help to take a major step to grow in your career. If you tolerate the current (situation) dissatisfaction, then you will not have any motivation to move to a higher platform. Hence, I consider that tolerance to the current dissatisfaction is one of the restraining forces.

It will be a good idea for every one of us to draw the above diagram with our driving forces and restraining forces. To move forward in life the obvious way is to increase the driving forces, viz increasing your level of motivation, improving your skill sets, increasing your qualifications, doing hard work / smart work, etc. This needs a lot of energy.

A smarter way is to focus on the restraining forces and see whether you can eliminate or weaken any of them. If you can achieve this, then the restraining forces will reduce. In such a case, with the same amount of driving force, you can have faster growth in your career.

Trust me, your success is in your hands.

CHAPTER EIGHTEEN

NEWTON'S THIRD LAW OF MOTION

I strongly believe that the 3 laws of motion postulated by Newton are very much related to our personal life as much as it relates to Physics. I dedicated a chapter each to the first law of motion and the second law of motion in my recently published book titled "French Fries - 15 golden ideas to power your career growth". The third law of motion is very popular and hence I did not cover it in that book.

The third law of motion stipulates that every action has an equal and opposite reaction. It can also be understood as every effect has got a cause that is responsible for that effect. Most of us believe that our current situation is the making of someone else. In most cases, it is not so. The situation in which we are in is because of something that we have done or not done in the past.

It is not uncommon to listen to someone blaming their current situation on their parents and their upbringing. While it can be sympathized with, I am sure you will agree that action from that person could have improved or changed the situation. Hence the inaction from that person is the cause of the current situation the person is in.

If a student has secured a lower grade in his exams, it is attributable to his ill preparation which is the cause of the effect. You can blame it on the question paper saying that the problem was difficult, the questions came from the chapter that you chose not to prepare, etc. But the truth remains, a better preparation could have improved the situation.

If one of the spouses does not commit quality time with the other person, there is no way that he or she can blame for a poor relationship. Not spending quality time is the cause of the result (poor relationship).

In the case of a professional environment, we would hear from many people that they have not been promoted or they have not been given a proper assignment by their superiors. But the individual has to find out what has caused this situation.

In most situations, we are the ones who caused the result. If we can identify what we have done (or not done) to be in this current situation it would help us to upgrade ourselves from the current situation.

Understanding the relationship between the Cause and the Effect will help us to build a better future.

CHAPTER NINETEEN

JUDGEMENTAL

We all know that it is not fair to be judgemental about a person or a situation. Thus said, it is extremely difficult to practice this.

We form impressions about people based on our past experiences with them. Sometimes we brand a certain section of a people as good or bad. Our interaction depends on this preconceived notion. It is very difficult to remove such a perception.

I get reminded of a line that I read in the book "7 Habits of highly effective people" which said, "What you are shouts so loudly in my ears, I cannot hear what you say". My boss had this sentence running on his computer screen, as a screensaver. This computer was placed on the adjoining table so that whenever he wants to work on his computer, he would turn around and work. Hence the display on the computer screen will be visible to the people who come to his room for any discussion. I'm not sure whether he kept this intentionally or not. Nevertheless, this used to caution me during my discussions with him. Accordingly, I will try my best to communicate in a manner that reaches him without any contamination.

I'm sure you would have also experienced situations wherein you felt that the person talking to you is going to say something against you, but it would turn out that he/she was appreciating you. This is because of your earlier experience with him/her or with someone like him/her. By becoming aware of the existence of such judgemental attitudes, we may be in a position to reduce such incidents in our life.

Having understood that it is very likely that we would be judgemental in most of our transactions, we should also realize that others with whom we communicate are also likely to be with such bias. Hence in any important conversation, it is essential to evaluate whether the other person is likely to have some bias towards us whether good or bad. Identifying such a bias will help us in structuring our communication with the other person. In case you feel that the other person is likely to have a negative bias towards you, it may be worthwhile to resolve that much ahead of any important conversation.

While it may be very difficult to avoid being judgemental, it'll be good to know that such a thing exists and we may not be an exception to it. Knowledge of such a bias can help in improving our transactions. It is often said that "what gets measured gets improved", similarly, "what gets diagnosed gets cured"

CHAPTER TWENTY

HAKUNA MATATA

Getting anxious in difficult situations is not uncommon for most of us. Every one of us wants to avoid such a situation and feel Hakuna Matata (roughly translates to "there are no troubles" or "no worries" in the Swahili language. This phrase became famous due to the movie "The Lion King").

Getting anxious, getting angry, and getting worried can only result in reducing our capability to handle the situation. Once I was talking to a friend of mine on this subject, and he suggested that I should listen to MS Dhoni who is referred to as a cool captain. In one of his videos, he mentions "I feel equally frustrated, angry, and disappointed at times, but what is important is that none of these is constructive. What needs to be done right now is more important than all these emotions". He further mentions that he focuses on the process than the result. Thinking about the results can put undue pressure on us, hence we should focus on controllable, which can help to improve the situation.

Let me share with you one of my experiences in my marketing career. I once visited the office of our customer to participate in a negotiation meeting to finalise an order for a large number of machines for their new project requirement. I was waiting to be called for negotiation. Our competitor was from Europe. There was an elderly person who was the marketing head of this European company, who was also sitting in that room waiting to be called. That was the first time that I met this person and as a normal behavior of most of us I greeted, "Good Morning". The person refused to respond and gave me a cold stare. After a while when I was called for the discussion, that person looked at me and said, "You will not get this order". I replied, "That's fine" and I added, "All the very best to you".

My junior colleague who accompanied me for this discussion was feeling very bad that we were wished bad luck. He was also upset that I wished "All the best". He told me that we should have also told that person, "You will not get the order". I told my colleague not to worry about it. Let us focus on activities and not what that person told us.

I could understand that my competitor was trying to create a negative emotion so that I feel weak during the discussions with my customer. I wanted to feel better and hence I wished "All the best". It made me feel better as a person.

The negotiation with the customer went on for several hours, till midnight. Finally, we succeeded in getting the order. I was very happy, not only because I got the order but also because I was able to handle the negative criticism very well.

Hakuna Matata!

CHAPTER TWENTY-ONE

MENTORING

The role of mentoring is a very special and an interesting role. As we grow in our profession, we are required to educate and train our juniors to do certain jobs. Each of us follows different methods of mentoring.

I would like to share an anecdote to showcase an excellent trait of a mentor.

One engineering college student from India had applied for an opportunity to work as a summer intern at a famous University in the US, in the area of robotics. He was granted the opportunity by the university. He landed in the US with lots of dreams. He met the Professor with whom he corresponded. The Professor allotted a project to him. Unfortunately, the skill set required for doing this project was different from the skill set that he had. He approached the Professor and told him, "It looks like there is an error in the allotment of the project because the skill set that I had mentioned in the application is different from the skill sets required for doing this project." The Professor asked him, "Why did you come here?" He replied, "I have come here to learn". The Professor said, "Then please do it". The professor also allotted a mentor to him. The student met the mentor and explained to him the situation and asked him, "How much time can I take to complete this project". The mentor replied, "You can take 25 days". The student asked again, "How much time would you take to complete this project". The mentor replied, "Probably 20 days".

The student told himself, "I should finish this project at least in 19 days". As a typical Indian student, he worked hard and completed the project in 12 days. He went to the mentor and told him, "I completed this project in 12 days. Having completed the project and having known your capabilities in the past 2 weeks, I am sure you can finish this project in 4 to 5 days. Why did you mention that it would take you 20 days to do this project?" The mentor replied, "Had I mentioned that I would take only 4 to 5 days, it would have put enormous pressure on you to complete the project and would have created frustration in you". He continued, *"as a mentor, my job is not to tell you how proficient I am in a job but to help you to learn and complete the job that is given to you".*

This is an excellent example of mentorship. Every one of us will come across situations wherein we will be required to train & develop youngsters in our company. When you are required to impart training to your juniors, please remember the above story and ensure that you do not boast of your capabilities, but rather motivate them to learn and complete the project. When the mentoring is done effectively and selflessly the mentee develops very fast. An organization that practices mentoring as a culture becomes a learning organization. When continuous learning is put into practice, it builds a great organization.

CHAPTER TWENTY-TWO

TAKE CARE OF YOUR BODY. IT'S THE ONLY PLACE YOU HAVE, TO LIVE

"Take care of your body. It's the only place you have, to live" I read this on a poster at my office. It is probably one of the most profound statements that I ever read. It clearly states the importance of our health. We would have heard or seen the following statement as well, "You spend your health to earn wealth, only to realise that you have to spend the wealth to make good the lost health".

While we give importance to our career growth, many of us ignore taking care of our health (physical & mental)

The people who work in the manufacturing industry will be aware of the terms; Preventive maintenance, Total productive maintenance, Autonomous maintenance, etc. These are philosophies and practices that are followed in a factory to ensure that the machines perform to their maximum potential and do not have emergency breakdowns.

It will not be a surprise if I say that human beings are the most complicated piece of machinery in the world. It is like a factory. It has several departments like in a factory, a pump house (heart), electrical wiring (nerves), a Programmable Logic Controller (brain), a purifier (lungs), a process industry (digestive system), etc. If we consider "preventive maintenance" as a key initiative for the proper functioning of the factory, it is a pity that we fail to realise the importance of Preventive Maintenance for our bodies.

Similar to the schedules that we have for "preventive maintenance" in the factory, we should have similar schedules for the upkeep of our health.

It is not the lack of knowledge that is keeping most of us away from taking care of our health but it is the lack of will that keeps us away from taking the initiative. As mentioned in one of my earlier chapters titled "Success Mechanism is a *normally closed* valve", we have a lot of resistance that keeps us away from taking an initiative. Overcoming this resistance is a skill. (In my book titled "French Fries", I have extensively dealt with how to overcome this resistance.)

I urge you to focus on the following areas to ensure that you take care of the "only place" where you have to live.

1. Give your body the much-required flexing; it can be in the form of jogging, exercise, playing swimming, yoga, etc.
2. Eat good food and not junk food
3. Read books that kindle your thoughts.
4. Travel to new places to widen your mind
5. Smile at people, appreciate and help people. Such deeds secrete Oxytocin. (Oxytocin is good for the heart and good for lowering our blood pressure. It is also believed

that it helps to increase the confidence of the person). *Moreover, you look beautiful when you smile and help people.*

CHAPTER TWENTY-THREE

DECISION ANXIETY

From the moment we wake up in the morning we are required to make several decisions, some of which are done at a subconscious level. Every action that we take or do not take, is a result of a decision made by us.

Getting up in the morning and going to the office is also a result of a decision because you have an option of not going to the office as well. Similarly, for a student going to college is also a result of a decision, as he or she has the choice of not going to college. But in such cases, it may sound like there is no other choice. It just means that the other option of "not going" is likely to have such a bad outcome that we feel "there is no option". These decisions may not cause much anxiety.

In our professional life, we are required to make several decisions. These decisions cause a lot of anxiety to us because we worry whether we are making the right decision or not. The stress or the anxiety in decision-making is due to the following reasons

1. We are not sure whether the outcome of the decision will be positive or negative.
2. The impact of a negative outcome could be disastrous.

Let's assume that you are preparing a tender document for your company. The decision of what price to quote is very critical as it decides whether your company will get this contract or not. Your anxiety level depends on the uncertainty of the positive outcome and the impact that it can cause on you/your company. In this case, the uncertainty is high because we are not aware of what the other bidders will quote. The impact of the outcome can also be big, as your company may end up at a loss without this order.

Whenever you are faced with such Decision Anxiety, analyse and understand the level of uncertainty and impact and plot it in one of the quadrants in the picture below.

Let us assume that the order is for a huge value and the company needs this order to keep its shops busy. The uncertainty and impact are very, and it will fall under Quadrant I (High Stress). In case this tender is of a small value and your company is currently overloaded, it doesn't matter if you get this order or not. In such a case it falls under Quadrant III (Low stress). When you find it is fitting into quadrant III, you can understand that you need not worry much.

0--------Impact of the outcome --------10

Quadrant II Moderate stress	Quadrant I High stress
Quadrant III Low stress	Quadrant IV Moderate stress

0 ------Uncertainty of a positive outcome-------10

Decision Anxiety Matrix

However, if you find the situation fits into Quadrant I, you need to find ways of increasing the certainty and reducing the impact of the outcome. You would have seen, in our elections, some of the leaders choose to stand in two constituencies so that they reduce the impact of losing in 1 constituency and reduce the uncertainty because they are contesting in 2 constituencies.

In the case of a student applying for higher studies, it is common to see that he or she is applying to multiple universities to reduce the impact of not getting admission. In the case of business, to reduce the impact of losing an order, normally people tend to increase the customer base and participate in more tenders.

Having a backup plan is another effective way to overcome Decision Anxiety. In case you are not able to reduce either uncertainty or impact, I suggest you follow what our Cool Captain MS Dhoni says. "Focus on the process and not the result". Focus on the areas that are under your control, thus improving the probability of a positive outcome.

CHAPTER TWENTY-FOUR

WALK THE TALK

It was the year 1980. I got admission to do my B Tech at the Motilal Nehru Regional Engineering College in Allahabad. My elder brother accompanied me for admission into this college. After completing the formalities of admission, we learned that the college will start functioning after two weeks and the students can stay in the hostel.

During our journey from Chennai to Allahabad on the Ganga Kaveri Express, we made friends with Havildar Subbiah who was also traveling to Allahabad. His posting was in Allahabad and he was staying in a house outside the army campus. He accompanied us to the university for admission. He offered that I could stay with him till the college opens, as he is only staying alone in Allahabad. I welcomed this suggestion because the ragging in the college was supposed to be very bad at that time.

Not only me, but 2 more students from Tamil Nadu also stayed with him. He was such a kind person.

My father was concerned that I should not get into bad habits like smoking and drinking. In a letter that he wrote to Havildar Subbiah, he thanked him for hosting me and requested Havildar to ensure that I don't get into bad habits like smoking. Havildar showed me this letter, however, he did not respond to my dad's letter for three weeks. Post that he replied as follows.

Dear Sir, your son is doing well. You had asked me to take care that he does not get into bad habits. I could not advise him not to smoke as I was smoking. After receiving your letter I stopped smoking for the past three weeks and now I have the courage and conviction to advise your son not to smoke.

This simple incident illustrates the character of a person who wants to walk his talk. I am sure all of you would have seen such people and we regard them with a lot of respect. Even in our professional environment, we must preach only what we practice. If you want honesty, integrity, and sincerity to be followed in your organization or your department, or your team, you must practice these attributes. It will be meaningless for a team leader or a department head to expect everyone to come on time, while he or she comes 15 mins late to the office. This is true with every expectation of ours whether it is with our spouse, children, or younger colleagues. Before we expect others to do something, let us do it ourselves.

CHAPTER TWENTY-FIVE

YOU DO NOT GET A SECOND CHANCE TO MAKE A FIRST IMPRESSION

We all know that we should never judge a book by its cover. Likewise, we should never judge a person by his or her appearance. Though every one of us wants to be fair in our judgement, at a subconscious level we have biases that lead us to judge people by their appearance.

As we cannot ignore this bias, one should dress appropriately for the job that he or she is doing. Before we start talking to a person, our appearance makes a certain impact which we call the first impression. This makes a strong opinion in the subconscious mind and the interaction is biased by this opinion, at least for a while. The impression may change after a while, based on how we perform further. But sometimes the available time is too short and is not enough to change the impression.

I remember an incident 20 years ago. I was Manager - Exports and was introduced to the President of our company, as a potential candidate to take forward the export initiative in North America. Unfortunately, I was not dressed at my best on that day. I entered the room where the President and my boss were present. The President looked at me and before even I started my presentation, he said, "I do not think he will suit this role". It was a big shock for me and I realised my mistake. My eyes got filled with tears and had great difficulty managing them. My boss Mr. ES Kumar relentlessly pursued the President and convinced him that I am the right candidate for this position. This took another 6 months, as I had to showcase my performance to prove myself. This could have been avoided, had I presented myself properly on that day.

It is not only true to individuals but also very much true to companies.

Let me narrate another incident that happened later. We received one of our prestigious orders from a customer in Brazil. The engineer in charge of that project Mr. Alberto Gallon told me, Arul, this is the first time that we are going to try equipment from your company. Please ensure that you get it right at the first instance itself and he added "You do not get a second chance to make a first impression". These words got etched in my mind and I try my level best to make the best impression at the first opportunity. When we make a very good first impression, unknowingly this becomes our benchmark. Anything less than the benchmark will make us feel bad and hence to maintain our standard we will continue to do our best every time. I have seen people who are obsessed with making their first impression the best impression. Over time it becomes their second nature and they always do their best every time. Ladies and gentlemen, never miss an opportunity to put forth your best version.

CHAPTER TWENTY-SIX

APPRECIATION

We are social creatures, and we crave recognition from others. Whether it is our family members or colleagues in the office, we look for recognition from others. I am not referring to monetary or career-related recognition. This type of recognition is possible in the professional setup but is not possible in our day-to-day dealings with friends, family, and colleagues.

This is where appreciation comes in very handy. Appreciation is a very powerful tool to make a strong relationship with people around you. I was lucky to have seniors, friends, and family members who were very good at this and their appreciation motivated me a lot.

For many of us, appreciating others does not come so easily. This could be due to jealousy or it could be out of a feeling of "what is there to appreciate" as someone is doing their job.

Appreciation doesn't need to be done only by the senior to the junior. It could be done between peers and even from juniors to seniors. This is also very important between family members. While it is a common sight to see parents appreciating their children, it is a bit rare to see children appreciating their parents. Children should not ignore this.

It can be observed that a relationship between husband and wife is stronger when they appreciate each other's achievements generously.

When you appreciate people for their achievements, it makes them happy and helps them to achieve more. I am sure that if we make the world around us happy, we also experience happiness as we are a part of the ecosystem.

Appreciation should be done with complete genuineness and sincerity, or else it will do more harm than good. By appreciating others, we are not depriving ourselves of our success and our growth. There is a lot of space in this world for the growth of everyone and if you are determined to grow there is nothing to stop you.

CHAPTER TWENTY-SEVEN

LEARNING NEVER GOES TO WASTE

During my college days, I felt that I would become a design engineer. However, life took me on a different path. I was recruited by HCL Limited through the campus interview and posted in their factory at Dehradun as a trainee in Machine Shop. After a few years, in the late 1980's I joined Larsen & Toubro as an Executive taking care of import and export procedures. Those were the days of import restrictions, hence it was not easy to import materials without having a license. It was a complicated procedure to get a license. We had to deal with the Chief Controller of Imports & Exports (now called the Directorate General of Foreign Trade), Customs Authorities, and the Reserve Bank of India. This job was not technical. My peers in the company looked down on me as my job appeared to be more clerical than technical. They called me a glorified clerk. Two years went by, I felt that I was wasting my time. I decided to quit. I wrote my resignation letter and went to meet my boss. As luck could have it, my boss told me that I am being transferred to technical purchase. I tore my resignation letter and continued in L&T. Several years later,

I was fortunate to become the Chief Executive of one of L&T's many subsidiaries.

When I look back, my two years working in Import & Export department gave me a rare knowledge of the economics of the country, Import & Export Policy, interpretation of customs notifications, the regulations of the Reserve Bank, etc. This proved to be a major strength in handling my role as the Chief Executive. The skill of reading & deciphering the Customs Act, Exim policy, Govt notifications, etc., stood in great strength when I negotiated contracts & agreements with customers and collaborators as the Chief Executive. This brings us to a point that whatever we learn never goes to waste, it comes back to you as great support at some point in time.

I get reminded of Steve Jobs learning calligraphy. As he did not like the course that he was studying, he quit the class and started attending the calligraphy class, which he loved. I believe this inspired him to introduce multiple typographies on the Macintosh computer. Later it became the standard for all software.

Let me also cite another example. You might have heard of Alexander Babu, a stand-up comedian (better known as Alex). He is one of the best and most decent stand-up comedians. He has a great passion for music which he learned during his younger days. He mixed his unique expertise in music with comedy and made a blockbuster show that no one can copy. The show is called "Alex in Wonderland". This is on Prime Video. I can assure you that the 2 hours program is a non-stop meaningful laughter.

Friends, never hesitate to learn something that comes your way or something that you are passionate about though it is not connected to your profession presently. This will come in handy to you someday or the other.

When you apply such learning to your profession it sometimes provides huge leverage that no one can emulate or copy. When you learn, you may not understand how it will help you at a later stage, but it will certainly help you to do a rock star performance like Alex at a later date.

CHAPTER TWENTY-EIGHT

LUCK OR LAOS

I am not sure whether to believe in luck or not. It can be debated for hours and days whether there is something called luck, or it is just a probability of events happening. Whatever it may be, I strongly believe that it is possible to increase the probability (luck) of an event by adhering to the following simple steps

Listening, keeping your **Antennas** up, seizing **Opportunities**, **Striving** to excel (LAOS)

"Getting admission into an engineering college in the late 1970s was not an easy task, since there were only a very few engineering colleges in the state, unlike now. Students with very high marks only got admission. I missed getting admission since my marks in the Pre-University exams were lower by a couple of percentage points. I joined B.Sc. with a Physics major in a local government arts college in Pondicherry. Ravindran, a friend of mine was also in a similar situation and he joined BSc Chemistry at the same college. We used to spend a lot of time together on campus. One day during lunch he asked me, "Arul, why don't we write our pre-university exam again and try to secure better marks so that we can get into engineering college at least next year? It was a very casual discussion.

Many friends in the group did not buy this idea. Only Ravindran and I took this seriously. There was nothing for us to lose by writing the exam again, so we went ahead. Both of us wrote the exam once again and secured very good marks which enabled us to get admission into an engineering college. Had I ignored his word of wisdom, my life would have been totally different. To date, I value that great moment that changed my life. I was happy that I **listened** to him, my **antennas** were up to receive that signal for doing something better, seized the **opportunity** to rewrite the exam, and **strived** hard to do the exams well.

On another occasion, I was working in a company called General Optics Asia Limited in Pondicherry. I loved the company, my job, and my seniors. However, the company was small and there was no scope for growth. One of my well-wishers in the company told me that I should look for better opportunities outside. This was registered in my mind well, though I did not take any proactive steps towards changing the job. Sampath, a colleague of mine brought me a paper cutting wherein Larsen & Toubro had advertised for Vendor Development engineers. Since my antenna was up to receive signals related to what was registered in my mind, I applied for this job. As I did well in the interview, I was offered a job in this great organization, which I never dreamt of. I was not hunting or looking for a job at that moment, it was casual information that I received from my colleague. Here again, I felt lucky, rather the LAOS theory worked. (Please do not google to find more on LAOS theory. This is the word coined by me to remember the concept)

I continued to practice this throughout my life. There were several opportunities I seized. In some of them, I failed and in some, I succeeded. The net result was growth.

Dear friends, listening is an art. Please listen with the intent to understand and not with the intent to reply. When you listen to something important to you, it registers in your subconscious mind. When it is registered in your subconscious mind, your antenna receives all related messages automatically. You would suddenly find that information related to what you registered in your subconscious mind is coming to you in plenty. This helps you to take the next step and strive hard to achieve your goal.

CHAPTER TWENTY-NINE

PREPAID AND NOT POSTPAID

We all aspire to grow in our professional and personal lives. To achieve this, we should have a clear plan and also a clear commitment of resources for executing the plan. Resources can be money, time, or energy. It can also be a combination of these. However, some of us dream of achieving a goal without having a plan and without committing resources for the same.

Let us take a well-known example in India, i.e. preparing for a competitive exam such as JEE for getting into IIT. In such a case, a person may join a coaching class that prepares the students for the entrance exams. Such coaching may start from the 6th grade or earlier. A student who is serious about it will take up this well-laid-out plan and commit his or her resources (money, time, and effort). The commitment of resources is a prepaid activity and not a postpaid activity. This means that you need to put in your time & effort before you get results. Does this not seem obvious? Everyone knows it. What is so special?

I agree with you that this is obvious. But when it comes to our career growth, we do not follow this pattern of prepaid. Unlike in the case of the IIT entrance exam, there are no clear guidelines or infrastructure available to upgrade ourselves. So, most of us expect something good to happen such as a promotion without having put in the necessary commitment from our side. I have heard people saying that "When I get promoted, I will do a better job". This will not happen. Promotion (or growth) is not a postpaid activity. You need to put your efforts first to gain a promotion. It is a prepaid activity.

Let us assume that a person who is working in a company targets to become the functional head from his current position as a member of the function. The planning phase for this is very critical and difficult as well. The road may not be very clear to reach the position that one target. Please consider the following in the journey of achieving your goal.

- Identify the qualification that is required for that position.
- In case you do not possess it, is it possible to qualify?

    - What are the resources that you need to commit, say money, time & effort?
    - What are the sacrifices that you need to do? For eg., reduced personal time since you will be required to attend classes, travel to college, etc.

- In case you are not able to further your qualification, for whatever reason, is there any other manner by which you can compensate for the lack of qualification?

    - In several instances, I have seen people who are less qualified for the position have successfully risen to the position by sheer hard work and personal education.

- What are the traits that are required for the heading function that you are targeting? Do you have it? If not, can you acquire it?

Above is an example to show what "prepaid" means. Dear friends, prepare a plan for yourself to reach the target you wish to achieve. Success & Achievement are prepaid activities, hence commit the resources required for the same. Do not expect results/growth for which you will pay later with your efforts.

CHAPTER THIRTY

Brain Teases

I am immensely fascinated by the functioning of the brain. It is probably the most complicated stuff that we have ever known. Despite its incredible capability, the brain also has certain limitations.

You may be aware that we have five basic sensory capabilities such as seeing, feeling, hearing, smelling, and tasting. All these five senses can send about 11 million bits[1] per second as information to our brain. Out of this, the eyes can send 10 million bits[1] per second of information. However, it is said that our brain is capable of processing only about 50 bits[1] per second. This means a huge amount of information that is seen by our eyes is not registered in our brains. We are processing a small portion of the information through our conscious minds. Some information may go into the subconscious mind without our knowledge.

You might have heard of the popular awareness test. Please google "Test Your Awareness: Do The Test". Check it out yourself.

Now comes the question, of whether what we see is really what we see. The reality is, we see what we want to see. This brings us to a point that all our observations and opinions are based on the insignificant portion of the information that we have received from our sensory organs. When multiple people see the same event, they also process only an insignificant portion of it based on their mindset. Hence this could lead to a major difference in opinion between people. The point that we need to realize is that there is always another opinion that could be different from our opinion because both people have processed only partial information. Hence it is quite possible that by having a frank and open discussion, we may arrive at a better understanding of any event.

Friends, do not rush to a conclusion as soon as you come across an event, and make that your strong belief. When you talk to a person please be in an open mind and believe that his or her side of the story could also be true. If such an approach is adopted it will help in resolving many conflicts.

[1] Reference Britannica

CHAPTER THIRTY-ONE

GAME NOT OVER

It is likely that most of us have encountered difficult phases at some point in our lives. Some of us were fortunate that we could recover from the difficult situation much sooner than others. In such a difficult situation, what helps us to tide over is the hope of a good future. Even when you feel that you have hit a wall, there is always a possibility of an opportunity. As the saying goes, when one door gets closed, God opens another door. I know it is not easy to keep hopes high when someone faces a wall.

I would like to share an anecdote. A younger family friend of mine who had completed engineering in India, went to the US to do his MS. After completing his MS he was trying to get a job in the US to continue his stay there. Despite his best efforts, he could not find a job. Several months passed by and the time was running out. He had to take a call on whether to remain in the US or to come back to India. Continuing to stay in the US without a job is not an option since he cannot extend his visa.

He did several menial jobs to get some cash to meet his daily needs. At one point he was working in a restaurant as a waiter for almost 2 months. One day a new waiter joined the restaurant and they were chatting in their leisure time.

He asked my friend about his background and my friend replied that he has done his MS in engineering at one of the decent US universities. The new waiter was surprised and said. “I am here since I have not done any degree but why the hell you are here as a waiter after doing your Master’s”. My friend replied that he did not get a job and hence he was doing this activity just to meet the daily expense. He also said that he has given up trying for a job and that probably in another 2 weeks, he would go back to India as there was no other option for him. The new waiter replied to my friend, “If you have not got a job it only means that you have not tried enough”. This sparked my friend and he started looking for a job more seriously by quitting his waiter job. As you could guess, he managed to get a job. He later established a company of his own in the US and employed many people.

The moral of the story is,

“The Game is not over until you’ve tried your best”. And

“The best is always yet to come till you have achieved your goal”.

The spark can come from anyone, including a stranger. Please get ignited.

CHAPTER THIRTY-TWO

THE LAW OF ATTRACTION

Humans are bestowed with a unique feature of the conscious and unconscious mind. Though we may feel that we are taking all our decisions consciously, you may be surprised to learn that most of our actions are directed by our unconscious mind. When we practice certain activities regularly, it moves from the conscious to the unconscious level and we do it without being aware of it. People refer to this as Muscle Memory. Most of you would agree that walking, eating, and even driving are some such activities.

In one of my earlier chapters, I mentioned how the brain teases us. As explained in that chapter, the processing capability of our brain is a small percentage of the data that is sent by our sensory organs, and hence our conscious mind processes only a marginal portion of the inputs that are received. However, our unconscious mind registers many signals that we are not even aware of.

The unconscious mind is highly powerful and if we can sink some of our thoughts into this unconscious mind, it works for us even without us knowing of it. When you desire something, your unconscious mind gathers data related to this and brings it to your conscious attention.

I'm not sure whether you experienced this or not. Whenever I bought a new car, suddenly I find plenty of cars on the road with the same model and color. I used to feel that suddenly people started buying the same color of the car as I have purchased. It is no secret that the same color of the car was running on the road even earlier, however, my mind was not looking at it. The moment I purchased a car of a particular color, the unconscious mind shows such cars.

If you want to achieve something, the person who could help you is the unconscious mind. At one point in time, I wanted to improve my capability to deliver lectures. As my desire grew, I started getting opportunities because my unconscious mind projected information related to it and the conscious mind grabbed it. Similarly, when I thought about writing a book, suddenly information related to this started flooding my way without any specific action by me. It is the unconscious mind which attracts such information and projects it into our brains.

In your professional environment, if you'd like to improve or introduce something new and you have a strong desire for the same, your unconscious mind starts working on this desire. It captures information related to this and brings it to the attention of the conscious mind, which otherwise would have crossed without your knowledge.

If you want to achieve something, please sink it into your brain and the unconscious part of your brain starts attracting all information related to it. This is the power of our brain, use it to achieve your goals.

CHAPTER THIRTY-THREE

The Level of Perfection is Contextual

The first chapter in this book is on "Perfection", where I explained that whatever we do should be perfect. Furthering on this topic, I would like to add the following.

The level of perfection is not an absolute target. It depends on the context in which an activity is carried out. For example, when someone asks you, "How much was the sales turnover of your company?", we could answer it as Rs. 10 Bn (for eg.). However, it is quite unlikely that the sales number was exactly Rs. 10 Bn. It could have been, say Rs 10,000,360,435/-. This is rounded off to Rs 10 Bn. In this context, it is good enough if you say it as Rs 10 Bn. Similarly, when a Doctor asks your weight, you may reply 65 kgs (for eg) and I am sure it could be inaccurate to the extent of 1 or 2 kgs. However, if you go to the store to buy gold, you need to be accurate to a milligram.

Several years ago, when I was in marketing, I was working on an estimation, based on which we needed to submit our quotation the next day. It is not unusual that we were running against time in such situations. My boss was following up with me whether I had finished the estimation. I was struggling with one of the items for which I did not have a reasonable estimate. I told my boss that I would finish it the next day. My boss replied, "It is too late" and asked me, "What is the problem?". I explained to him the situation and he told me, "Arul, I understand that the estimation will not be accurate/perfect without the information that you are still struggling to get, however, the impact of this imperfection is insignificant to the whole purpose for which we are working. Please understand that perfection is contextual, and it is not an absolute target to achieve, it varies depending on the purpose."

This clarification regarding the level of perfection was quite revealing to me in the early years of my professional career. This helped me to complete the job with the perfection required for the purpose. Initially, it was difficult as I struggled to identify the level of perfection required for a job. As we go through such situations, again and again, we perfect the art of identifying the level of perfection required for the purpose.

CHAPTER THIRTY-FOUR

AMYGDALA

If you read about the brain, you will be fascinated by an almond-shaped object called Amygdala. Through this Amygdala, emotional responses are initiated. It also plays a pivotal role in carrying our memories. To understand how our brain functions, for eg., let me list down typical activities carried out in our brain when our eyes see an object.

- A visual signal first goes from the retina to the thalamus (a part of our brain)
- It is translated into the language of the brain (maybe an electrical signal)
- This signal goes to the visual cortex (another part of the brain) where it is analyzed and assessed for meaning and appropriate response;
- If that response is emotional a signal goes to the Amygdala to activate the emotional centers.

Sometimes the time taken by the brain to process an input and provide a response may be a bit longer than what a situation warrants. For example, let us imagine that you're walking in a garden, and you see a snake that crosses your leg just an inch away from your foot. The natural reaction would be to jump and get away from that place. Let us see what happens in our brain

- The eyes capture the image of the snake
- It is sent to Thalamus,
- In Thalamus it gets converted into a signal
- Then it is sent to the visual cortex,
- It analyses and decides on an action and sends the signal to Amygdala
- Amygdala instructs action for us to run away from the situation.

Though all these take place in milliseconds, it is sometimes too late for a given situation. Hence our brain is equipped with a shorter emergency circuit, which happens as follows

- A smaller portion of the original signal goes straight from the thalamus to the amygdala. Here, Amygdala compares this input with a similar situation in the past and gives urgent instruction to react. Thus, Amygdala can trigger an emotional response before the Cortex centers have fully understood what is happening. Amygdala can trigger a response in half the time than what the normal function of the brain takes.
- You might have experienced that we mistakenly assumed a rope to be a snake and jumped. This happens because the image of the rope which is observed by the eyes is sent to the rear part of the brain for processing and at the same time to the amygdala. The amygdala roughly compares it with similar images it has got in the memory and assumes it to be a snake and instructs you

to jump. Shortly thereafter the brain through its normal process finds out it is a rope and not a snake and we feel relieved.

You may be wondering why I'm talking about the amygdala here. In our daily life, sometimes we are not able to control our reactions to another person. Such an emotional reaction is also initiated by the amygdala by its emergency reaction circuit before the center of the brain could process the inputs and provide a correct reaction. If only we allow a few seconds more to react we will most probably get a properly processed reaction for that situation. Just by allowing a few extra seconds to process our reactions, we will greatly benefit from the capability of our brain to a proper reaction, else we become a slave of the Amygdala's emergency response which is designed by nature to take care of the emergency and not for reacting to people during discussions.

CHAPTER THIRTY-FIVE

THE MASTER EQUATION

I was fascinated by the below master equation which explains in a very simple manner how our Happiness / Success / Performance is related to our capabilities and attitudes.

(IC + AC) * A = H/P/S (Happiness or Performance or Success)

IC – Inborn capability

AC – Acquired capability

A - Attitude

(I did not coin this equation. I read it in a book. I am not able to recall where I read this.)

Our capabilities can be classified into 2 categories. Inborn capabilities and Acquired capabilities.

Inborn capabilities are something that comes with us when we are born. There can be a debate about whether we are bestowed with special skills when we are born. Some don't believe in this. Have we not heard of the child prodigy? In Wikipedia, a **child prodigy** is defined as a person under the age of ten who produces meaningful output in some domain to the level of an adult expert.

Some children are gifted with certain Inborn capabilities that enable them to perform at a level of an expert. Extending this belief: if a child can be born with extraordinary capabilities (let us put a number to it as 100), I believe that every child is born with various shades of capabilities, from high capabilities to low capabilities (i.e. varying from 100 to 0). It is just that we do not realise it since it is not extraordinary like that of a Child Prodigy.

Acquired capabilities are something that we acquire during our life. This could be through formal education in school and college or informal learning from our friends, colleagues, and elders.

Attitude is something that converts our capabilities into our desired results, namely happiness or performance, or success. You could have come across people who have immense capabilities (both Inborn and acquired) but a poor attitude in converting their capabilities into actions that could result in their success.

It does not matter if you're not born with a high level of Inborn capabilities. From the equation cited above, you could understand that if you are not blessed with inborn capabilities you may have to put more effort to increase the Acquired Capabilities. What matters is the sum of inborn and acquired capabilities. When these capabilities are put to use through a proper attitude then you can achieve what you desire.

CHAPTER THIRTY-SIX

SCRIPT

You must have heard about the word "Script", which represents the way the characters are expected to play their roles in a movie or a drama. "Script" also refers to a software programming language. The word "Behavioral Script" is used to explain how a person or a group of people behave in a given situation repetitively.

I would like to share a concept that I refer to as "Script" which many of us use knowingly or unknowingly. In your day-to-day life, you can observe that a Script is used by the mother on the child, husband on the wife, and wife on the husband. What I am referring to is, that when you repeatedly tell a person that he/she will behave in a certain manner, it scripts the person's behavior in that manner. You could have observed in a social gathering, a wife mentioning that her husband does not get angry with her. When such a statement gets repeated often in public it slowly embeds in the mind of the husband that he shall not get angry. This is also applicable in the reverse order when a husband mentions the behavior of his wife in a repeated manner.

Similarly, when a mother or father talks about their child in public, when the child is around, that the child is very responsible, it brings in the change in the child to become more responsible. This is a very positive way of bringing a change in a person. While this works positively it also works negatively. When you repeatedly tell a person that he will behave in a bad manner then you are sculpting the person to behave as per your script.

This is also applicable to our professional environment. When a Team Leader mentions in public that his team always gives importance to the team's success over an individual's success, the team's behavior goes as per this script. It is important that such statements are made when the team exhibits at least some shades of such behavior, then only it can reinforce that behavior. If a Team Leader makes such a comment when there is complete disarray in the team, it does not work.

If we continuously sculpt the world around us with a positive script, we can make the world a more peaceful and enjoyable place for all of us.

PS: I do not know whether "Script" is defined in psychological or sociological spheres in this manner. Please do not bother about it. I am just trying to get across a simple idea of how we can influence good behavior in a person.

CHAPTER THIRTY-SEVEN

METACOGNITION AND METAMOOD

In my earlier chapter on the Amygdala, I explained how an emotional reaction initiated by the amygdala results in an emotional outburst. In this chapter let me explain how to overcome this emotional outburst.

I would like to talk about metacognition and metamood. Metacognition refers to awareness of thought processes and metamood refers to awareness of one's own emotions. Let me not bother you with these high-sounding words. We can replace these words with the well-known terminology "self–awareness," which means knowledge of onc's internal states.

Managing emotions is one of the most difficult jobs for almost everyone. In most cases, we are not under our own control when emotions rage. We can classify people into three states when he or she is handling emotions.

Engulfed

These people are totally under the control of their emotions. Normally they come to an understanding of what they did (when they were emotionally swamped) after they regain their emotional stability.

Accepting

These people are clear about what they are feeling but they tend to accept their mode and so they do not change. For example, people who feel depressed.

Self-aware

These people are aware of their moods when they are undergoing that mood. Due to this awareness, they can ensure that their reactions are within certain boundaries and can control their outburst. Their self-awareness also helps them to get out of their bad mood quickly.

I read the above explanation in the book Emotional Intelligence by Daniel Goleman. This is one of the most interesting and informative books that I have read.

After reading this book I started observing myself during my emotional outbursts. Initially, I remembered my resolve of observing myself only after the emotional outburst has crossed. By reminding myself continuously I slowly became aware of my anger/emotional status. This means that I was going through an emotional outburst and at the same time I was aware that I am angry. This was the tipping point.

Through continuous practice, my awareness of anger became stronger and stronger, and, in most cases, I was able to control the anger. In certain situations where I am required to show my displeasure (by being angry), I could do it by pretending to be angry but the emotions were under my control. (I do not want to debate whether pretending to be angry is the right approach or not. I leave it to your judgment.)

I urge you to observe yourself when your emotions are taking over you. Please observe, don't try to control it. Soon you will move towards metamood status and control your reactions to that situation.

Welcome to the meta world.

CHAPTER THIRTY-EIGHT

ROLE MODEL

In the early years of my corporate career, I was told to identify a Role Model so that I look at him/her for shaping my career. I did not know how to select a role model. I thought role models should be well-known names, like Gandhi, Nelson Mandela, Ratan Tata, and the like. But I did not understand what I should do with such big names as role models. As the years went by, I realized that the role models are to be taken from the areas where I would like to grow. Hence, I identified Mr. AM Naik Chairman of Larsen & Toubro as my role model. For a while, I felt very proud that I have an iconic figure as my role model. Soon I realized that it was not helping me, I hardly had the opportunity to observe him closely to understand his way of working. I realized that the purpose of having a role model is to imbibe the qualities that I would like to practice to achieve my ultimate goal. Having Mr. Naik as a role model certainly gave me a lot of drive for pushing myself but did not help me learn from him. Having a role model is to observe how he handles an issue/ function/ relationship and learn from it. Merely keeping Mr. Naik, Mr. Narayanamurthy, or Mr. Chandraseker as role models cannot help us to improve ourselves.

Later I realized that it is not necessary to have one person as a role model. It would be better if we identify the areas that we want to improve and select persons who are good in those areas. I identified areas where I need to improve such as Customer Relations, Networking, Business Acumen, and Technical competence. For each of these categories, I identified people who were good in those areas and whom I could observe closely. For example, Mr. ES Kumar, who was the Chief Executive of the unit where I worked, was very good at maintaining customer relations. His approach used to be simple. Mr. NS Sivaraman who was my boss for a long period was good at networking and maintaining relationships. Mr. Subbu who was heading the Machinery business at L&T was good at promoting products and building efficiency in the organization. Whenever I take some initiatives, I recall how they would handle such initiatives. In my initial years of marketing, Mr. Lakshminarashimhan was my boss. He was respected in the market for his technical competence. I admired him for this. Throughout my career, I ensured that my technical competence in the product was good, though there were experts to explain this to the customers. It did earn respect for me.

Dear readers, identifying people who were good in the traits that I wanted to imbibe and whom I was able to observe continuously helped to improve myself, Why not you?

CHAPTER THIRTY-NINE

I AM IN RECEIPT OF YOUR MAIL ....

Many times, we look for big things in life and miss out on basic & simple things that are required to build our personal and professional life. Many of us attend training programs on teamworking, interpersonal skills, negotiation skills, marketing strategies, etc to grow in our professional and personal life. While we take steps to learn these aspects, we might miss out on basic hygiene factors of the business relationship or team working, such as acknowledging an email, honoring simple commitments, returning a call, being punctual, etc.

I get reminded of my initial experience in developing export markets for our machines. After the initial success in South East Asian and South American markets, we conducted a survey to understand what was that the customer liked in us which resulted in placing orders on us instead of their regular supplier of machinery from the United States. This questionnaire had a set of questions to answer on a scale of 0 to 10 and had an open-ended question asking for the one thing that they liked most in our business relationship. More than 50% of the respondents replied that the one thing that they liked most in our business relationship was, our immediate response to their messages/emails.

On that day I learned how important it was to respond to a mail immediately. Honestly speaking, I was responding immediately due to my enthusiasm to build the export market for our products and not because someone will measure this. Arising out of this learning, I made it a point that I would respond to all relevant emails within 24 hrs.

I continued to practice it to date by replying to the emails with appropriate answers or letting them know that I have received the mail and will respond by so and so time. I find this to be a very simple habit that has a great impression on the other person. This also helps in being a responsible team player and enhances our personality.

Some people don't acknowledge having received the mail though they may be working on the mail and preparing an answer which may take them a few days. When the sender does not get a response, it leaves him wondering whether the receiver is working on the mail or not. Unknowingly it creates a negative impression. We must indicate that we are working on the mail and will respond by such and such date.

I strongly feel that these skills (which I refer to as hygiene factors) are very essential for growth. If you ask me, "Is it not possible to grow in a professional career without these skills?". Hmm..., I would say "growth becomes easier with these skills, and more importantly, sustaining the growth is easier when your foundation is strong with such hygiene factors.

CHAPTER FORTY

TO BE OR NOT TO BE

As you might know, "to be or not to be" is a famous quote from William Shakespeare's work. This is probably the most famous soliloquy (speaking to oneself aloud) in literature. Please do not get worried, I am not going to talk about literature.

I am going to talk about the learnings from our bosses. In our professional career, we may come across many bosses, some tough and some soft, some arrogant and some kind, some knowledgeable and some not so knowledgeable, some effective and some not so effective. Whatever it may be there is something to learn from each of them.

I worked with several bosses. From some, I learnt things that I should do and with others, I learnt things that I should never do. To put it differently, I learnt whether **To be** one such person or **Not to be** one such person. In my experience, there is no one in this world from whom we can not learn something to do or not do.

It is very common to cite examples of what we have learnt **to do** from our bosses. I would like to cite examples of my negative learnings, i.e. things that I should never do. I had a boss who would never listen to others. He will not even entertain anyone to share their opinion with him. Even if someone muster the courage to share thoughts with him, he would put him down so badly that he will not talk again. Though he was a very intelligent person, this trait of his resulted in wrong decisions for the organization, which could have been avoided if he was receptive to others' ideas. This was a very strong lesson I learnt i.e. to listen to others and importantly, never put down a person when he is sharing something with you.

Sometimes I was required to take him to meet our customers. Even while dealing with customers he never was receptive to them. Whenever the customer proposed something, he would rebut with something opposite. He might be technically right but grossly wrong concerning winning/ maintaining a relationship.

I had another boss, who was very sweet to everyone. One of the finest gentlemen. He will never hurt anyone's feelings. But this trait of his did not allow him to take tough decisions which were required for the organization. This put the company's growth in trouble. I learnt that being Nice at the cost of the organization's objectives is not correct.

Finally, To be or Not to be, is the most important question in our learning from others.

CHAPTER FORTY-ONE

COMPETENCY

About 4 years ago, I was chatting with a consultant. He asked me, “Are you doing anything apart from your professional job?”. I said, “Nothing specific, except reading books and supporting some NGOs”. He asked, “You have decades of experience in the corporate world and why don’t you share your knowledge with youngsters”. I said, “I am in a general management function and there is nothing much I can share”. He replied, “Arul, this is the problem with many of us, we do not know what we know” and he explained to me about the levels of competence.

1. Unconscious incompetence
2. Conscious incompetence
3. Conscience competence and
4. Unconscious competence.

He explained, that initially, we are not aware of what we do not know. Then, we discover what we do not know and we are conscious of our ignorance of it. As a third step, we learn that skill and consciously perform the task. The final stage is that it becomes our second nature and we exhibit that skill unconsciously. To cite an example; at a younger age, we are not aware that we need to learn to drive. As we grow into our middle teens, we understand that it is essential to learn to drive. We become conscious of it. Then we learn to drive and drive a vehicle with a conscious effort in maneuvering it. After a year, driving becomes so easy that we maneuver the vehicle almost unconsciously. This is the unconscious competence level. It is like Sachin Tendulkar playing cricket.

The consultant told me, "The very fact that you are handling a company well for many years means that you certainly have a competence in it that could be shared. It is just that you are not aware of what you are aware of". I said, "Maybe, but I do not have the writing skill". He asked, "Who said that?". I said, "No one, but ...". He told me, "Many people do not even know that they have a skill which is inherent in them or learnt unconsciously. For example, you have learnt to write in primary school, and you have been writing several pages during school and college days. Now you are continuing to write as you communicate for business reasons. For years, you have been continuously learning and honing this skill. For all you know, you may be good at writing. Please explore it."

This was an incident that helped me to discover my ability to write and author my first book "French Fries – 15 Golden Ideas to power your career growth"

Ladies and gentlemen, each one of you have competence consciously or unconsciously built over several years. Explore your competence and create a new expression of the same. There are several examples of this. If you had watched Airtel Super Singers Season 7 (Tamil), you may be aware of Mukuthi Murugan and Sam Vishal. They had accidentally identified their singing ability and ended up as Winner and a second runner-up respectively.

They were neither singers by profession nor music was their hobby before attending the competition. The identification of their skills has changed their life forever. I am sure many skills are residing in your unconscious level, bring them to the forefront and enjoy your new avatar.

CHAPTER FORTY-TWO

MAGIC OF COMPETITION

In the early 1990s when India launched its liberalization initiative, many Indian companies embarked on growing the export market. I was a Purchase executive then. I was transferred to export marketing and asked to promote exports aggressively.

In one of my regular sales calls in the South East Asian market, I met the Director of one of the largest tyre makers in the world, at his Singapore office. In our casual talk, he asked me where am I coming from. I told him that I am coming from Thailand after a meeting with his competitor. I also told the name of the company. He said, "We do not consider that company as our competitor". I asked, "Why so, they are also as big as you are, with several billion dollars in sales". He replied. "you are right, but they are no match for us in terms of quality". I felt that he was being arrogant, and I asked him, "Are you saying you do not have competition". He said, "We consider "so and so" company as our competitor since their product quality is as good as ours". He added, "It is because of them our quality is good". I asked, "Why do you say so", I did not have the guts to ask him, “Do you copy them”. He said, “Since they also make good tyres, it puts pressure on us to improve and stay ahead. We certainly want competition in our market. If there is no competition, there will be no product innovation”.

It was interesting for me to hear this.

This is not only true to the business environment but is also applicable to individuals.

When the company for which I was working decided to embark on exports they transferred me to Export marketing. Initially, I was a one-man army. After seeing the initial success in Asia and South America, the management decided to hire one more person. I was not aware of this. Suddenly there was a circular that Mr. Sarath is joining as an Export Marketing Executive. I was worried, am I losing my job? I asked the same question to the chief executive to whom I was reporting. He said, “Arul, I am quite happy with your performance. However, to expand the export market, it is necessary to have one more person”. I asked him, “Sir I'm looking after the complete export market and what will Sarath look after”. He laughed at my naïve question and said, “There is only one world, so let us split it into two. You look after Asia and South America and he will look after Europe and North America”. From his point, it was a very simple decision. I felt as though my property was snatched and given to someone else. Sarath came with an MBA degree from a proper B school whereas my background was BE with an MBA through distance education. The mere presence of Sarath put me under pressure. Introducing a competition suddenly changed the way I looked at work. I put extraordinary efforts to grow my market. I worked till late at night, talking to my customers in South America to get more orders and to prove that I am better than Sarath. This made me understand that competition not only improves the performance of the companies but also the individuals. Hence, be happy if there is competition for you. It will help you to hone your skills and improve your performance.

CHAPTER FORTY-THREE

SMALL ACT, BIG IMPACT

When a bee sits on a flower and drinks the nectar the pollen gets stuck to its body. When the bee goes to another flower the pollen gets transferred to that flower resulting in pollination. The bee is not aware of the great help that it is rendering to the plant kingdom by its involuntary action.

Likewise, each of us can create a huge impact on others' lives through our involuntary actions. I am not going to talk about what I did to others, but rather what others did to my life involuntarily.

I was academically a poor student in my school days. By the time I reached the 7th standard, I changed 6 schools, all were Tamil medium Government schools. My parents decided to put me into a good school, but it was not easy due to my poor academic record. Mr. Dawood Reddiar, my Dad's friend spoke to Father Peter (the school Principal and his friend) and secured admission for me to the best school in Pondicherry. This was a turning point in my life. (help traveling beyond religions, a Muslim person recommending a Hindu boy to his Christain friend)

Though I secured decent marks in 11th standard, Vivekananda College, Chennai was reluctant to give me Maths, Physics & Chemistry group in PUC (the equivalent of 12th std). They gave me the Biology group. I was extremely poor in Biology. My Dad's friend Mr. Vaithiyalingam, through his contacts, helped me to get Maths group. Vivekananda College brought out the best in me.

My marks in PUC were a little short of the cutoff for Engineering college admission (in those days there were only about 2000 seats in Tamil Nadu). I joined BSc in Physics at a local college. Ravindran, a classmate of mine suggested that we write the PUC exam again. I was unaware that such a thing was possible. He bought the application for me. Both of us wrote the exams and cleared with very good marks, good enough to join engineering. Had he not given me this suggestion, my life would have been different.

I was working in a startup company in Pondicherry. I enjoyed working there. Since this was a small company, the growth prospects were limited. Sampath, a colleague of mine brought a newspaper cutting wherein L&T had advertised for a vendor development engineer. I applied for this position and eventually joined L&T. 25 years later I ended up as the CEO of L&T Kobelco, a subsidiary of L&T.

While we remember the voluntary contributions of our parents, teachers, friends, etc, it is important to remember the small acts done by others that changed our life significantly. In my case, Dawood, Vaithiyalingam, Ravindran, Sampath, and many more helped me to be what I am. Remembering their contributions to my life makes me understand, that "what I am is not just my own making". It is a result of the small and big acts of many. I am sure they have no clue of what impact they caused on my life by their simple act. I am grateful to them.

A small help (sharing information, appreciating/ guiding someone, charity to the needy, etc) can provide a big impact on others. Hence do not miss an opportunity to help others even if it is a small help. This will create a better world for us to live in.

CHAPTER FORTY-FOUR

ENOUGH IS ENOUGH

Many times, we cling to some practices or ideologies that we very well know are not yielding the required results. For example, we stay in an area and commute to work for over 1 hour daily just because we are used to that area. Though there is a possibility of staying closer to the office we get used to the difficulty and do not attempt to try out a new area.

We buy material from a vendor though we know he is not reliable in terms of delivery. This vendor may require constant follow-up. We continue to buy from this vendor instead of changing the vendor. Over a period, we get used to it and feel it is okay to be so.

It is time to say, "Enough is Enough" and move on.

Long ago, when I was marketing custom-built capital equipment it was normal to dispatch the machine though there were some shortages so that the company meets the sales target. These used to be some small parts that do not hinder the installation and commissioning. Since the transportation, installation, and commissioning of the machine would take about a month, the company would arrange these short-supplied items and send them to the site. This was a nuisance since someone must follow up on these items. In most cases, this activity will get a second priority.

One day our boss decided that “enough is enough” and no more. He told us no equipment will be dispatched if there was a missing item, at the same time, he mentioned that he cannot tolerate a shortfall in our targets. This attitude of his made a big difference. Everyone in the supply chain understood that there is no option to dispatch the machine with short supplies and accordingly the vendor follow-up changed and from that time onwards the machines were despatched without any shortages.

This is not only applicable to the business situation it is also applicable to our personal life. A daughter of my friend joined a reputed tier 2 college in Chennai for doing her engineering degree. She found that the college does not encourage learning and the faculty was not good. She quit college after 1 year. She again wrote the competitive exams and secured admission to one of the most reputed colleges. She is doing extremely well in the US now. But for her bold step, she would not have grown the way she did.

In our lives, we could come across many such situations wherein we hesitate to decide to change the situation. Please take the courage to say “Enough is Enough” and take steps to change it. Once you decide to make a change, your mind will find ways to accomplish it.

This is also applicable to Governments. There are many things the governments are dabbling with that require courage and conviction to say “Enough is Enough”. For example, I wish the Indian government would make a strong ban on all plastic bags. Likewise, I wish the US government says “enough is enough” on their existing Gun policy soon.

CHAPTER FORTY-FIVE

CHALLENGES

Everyone faces challenges in their life. At a young age, when studies were our predominant challenge. As we grew, the challenges came in different forms. It could be on account of health, relationship, finance, career, professional rivalry, etc. We find ways and means of overcoming such challenges. For eg.

- People with physical challenges develop fantastic abilities in other areas that are difficult for others to match. Hence, they are referred to as Differently Abled.
- When there is a need to complete a job within a specific time, the mind finds ways and means of meeting this target.
- When a person decides on committing an EMI for buying a house, he finds ways and means of reducing his expenses.
- When a company goes through difficult times in terms of profitability (for eg), several measures are taken to reduce costs.
- When the market for a product shrinks the company comes out with new techniques to boost sales.

What does this mean? We are at our best when we are faced with challenges. We are alert, we look for new ways, we plan meticulously, etc. When we do a routine job, generally we are not giving our best.

You must have heard the term 'move out of your comfort zone". When you stay in your comfort zone, you do not give your best. If you want to bring out the best in you, please do not sit in your comfort zone.

Please grab new opportunities, after due diligence, though you might not feel comfortable with them. Please be assured that the discomfort enhances your performance. I mentioned "after due diligence" because some people take up new jobs without evaluating whether it is suitable for them or not. In such a case that person may land up in deep trouble. A friend of mine moved from the Computer Hardware industry to the fashion industry, where he had no experience or skill. This brought down his career, from which he could never recover.

Does this mean that we should regularly change our jobs to make us uncomfortable? Not necessarily.

Please evaluate your mindset now. Are you in a comfort zone? If yes, most probably you are not at your best. In most organizations, the demand for improvement on a year-on-year basis is a must. This is the way they try to bring out the best in people.

As you know, there is no limit to creativity and excellence. What was BEST yesterday is no more the BEST today. As they say, "Records are made to be broken". If there is a continuous craving for improvement in whatever area you are working on, it will create a positive discomfort or positive dissatisfaction. Such positive dissatisfaction works as a catalyst to make improvements. If you do not work on such dissatisfaction positively to improve yourself, it may lead to disappointment and depression. Hence be cautious in using this to improve yourself.

CHAPTER FORTY-SIX

ARJUN, EKLAVYA AND YOU

Ms. Bharathi Baskar, (a well-known "Tamil Debate Club speaker), in one of her lectures, explained how Lord Krishna could preach Bhagavat Gita to Arjun which runs into 18 Chapters, while the whole Gaurava troupe and Pandava troupe are standing one against the other to start the war. Under normal circumstances, it would have taken several days to preach it. Ms. Bharathi Baskar explained that between a good teacher and an extraordinary student, there is no need to use words to teach. The mere bonding between them establishes a media whereby the transmission of knowledge takes place.

You may have heard of the character Eklavya in Mahabharat. Dronacharya, the Guru for Royals, refused to teach archery to him. However, he still learnt by keeping Dronacharya's idol and practiced archery with great devotion. This helped him to master archery.

We may not be Arjun or Eklavya neither our bosses are Lord Krishna or Dronacharya. Then how do we learn?

Learning technical subjects are relatively easier since they are mostly taught through work instruction and practice. But the management cannot be taught through work instructions. Then how do we learn management?

Similar to how we learn about the life, by observing our elders, we can learn management by observing the actions of the boss and their corresponding results.

I worked with Mr. ES Kumar who was heading our unit as its Chief Executive. He was shrewd in marketing and business. He does not teach his principles. However, the strategy that he followed in marketing and business was so simple that it was easy for someone who is closely working with him to understand. It hardly required any big explanation. His simple philosophy was to meet and exceed customer expectations within ethical and legal means.

Not all bosses use simple strategies. Even if the bosses do not teach or do not use an explicitly identifiable strategy, I feel it can be learnt if you make effort to observe and learn.

Just don't observe only your boss, please observe your peers, sub-ordinate, and bosses of other departments.

P Kailas was my senior colleague in L&T. He was marketing Defence products and I was marketing Rubber machinery. (he later became MD of Shibaura Machine India Private Limited). We were seated in the same office. It is a pleasure to watch Kailas talking to the customers. He will make the customers feel that they are very important and also make them feel that they are in safe hands. Though he was never my boss, I observed him very closely and learnt marketing management from him.

CHAPTER FORTY-SEVEN

DECISIONS ARE SITUATIONAL

When I go to a temple or a shop with my wife, normally I drop her near the entrance and I will join her after parking the car in an available parking slot. When we are done with our prayers/ shopping and head towards our car, invariably my wife will find a free parking slot much closer than where I had parked. She will ask me, "Why didn't you park the car here instead of parking it far away". Honestly, this slot was not available when I parked. I will tell her the same. Till today I do not know whether she accepted my explanation. This is a conversation we have every time we go out.

I get reminded of a story called "The Lunatic" that was part of my 10th standard lesson. This was about a small automotive workshop (showroom) in Europe that specialized in modifying cars. Kindly note this story was written 50 years ago. This company was on the brink of closure as they ran out of orders. At that time a person walks in and orders a luxury car conversion. This seemed to be an opportunity for their survival. They jumped at this opportunity, borrowed funds, and made a fantastic car, without even seeking an advance from the customer. They asked the gentleman to come after a couple of weeks. The owners of the store continued to wait for several weeks but no one turned up. On enquiring about this gentleman, they found that the guy was a lunatic from the neighbouring town. However, as this sparkling car was parked in the showroom for weeks, it attracted many visitors and kindled their desire for a new car. The story ends by saying the showroom recovered to its past glory. If you evaluate the decision taken by the company, it will certainly look stupid as they ventured into making a luxury car without even verifying the background of the person who ordered it. It should be seen with the emotional backdrop of the owners who were looking for a small log of wood to save them from drowning.

A company known to me is into the manufacture of capital equipment. Eight years ago they were almost on the brink of bankruptcy. They had no orders for execution. They had only one inquiry that was under negotiation with a new customer from Sri Lanka. Apart from this inquiry, there were none. This customer refused to give advance payment and demanded many unreasonable conditions. Like in the above story of The Lunatic, this company was looking for a log of wood to keep floating. They took this order backed up by LC which helped them to borrow working capital from the bank and to keep themselves afloat. Once the equipment was ready, after 10 months, the Sri Lankan company postponed the delivery of the machine by 6 months. During this period of 1 year, the tides turned, and the company was flooded with others. However, the internal audit that came for auditing the company, made an adverse remark on the management that the company took an order without advance.

Please understand that the decisions are taken based on the realities & data available at the time of taking the decision. If it is evaluated on current realities it may not look appropriate. This is a dynamic world, what was correct yesterday may not look to be correct today. So, whenever you judge someone else's decision, please do not evaluate it with today's realities.

CHAPTER FORTY-EIGHT

DOING AND OWNING

The company where I worked, started a factory in China 15 years ago. A colleague of mine was transferred to this factory in China. When I met him after a year, I asked him about the work culture in China. He said that they were very obedient and would do whatever we ask them to do, without asking any questions. But, for some reason, if they are not able to do what has been told, they will stop the work and keep quiet. They will not even report. For eg., if the job of assembling a machine is given to them and there is some issue in the assembly, they will stop it and keep quiet. When asked, why they have not reported, I believe, they said "You did not tell us to report when there is a problem". They simply follow the instructions.

This scenario will occur when people are not owning a job. However, most people, when faced with a problem, they try to complete the job based on their experience and whatever is within their limits.

But, when people own the job, they find ways and means of completing the job, even if it is required to go beyond their actual area of control. They seek the right help and support to complete the job.

When I was handling export marketing, I received an inquiry from a customer in Malaysia for 10 nos. of machinery to be delivered in 3 months. The standard delivery period was 6 months. I approached our unit head and mentioned to him, "Sir, we have an enquiry for 10 machines with a 3 months delivery. Since our standard delivery term is 6 months, I am going to regret it". He asked me, "Arul, do you own your job or you are doing your job". I did not understand what he meant. I answered, "Sir, I have done my job of generating the enquiry, but the production needs more time, what can I do". He said, "You said it. "You have done your job". It means you are not owning the job. If you own the job, you will not conclude without making a full effort to meet customer requirements". He continued, "I suggest that you convene a meeting of production, engineering, and purchase teams and explain to them the importance of the order. (If we get this order, it would be a breakthrough with a global customer with a potential of over 100 nos of the machine) .

As suggested, I convened a meeting and explained the importance of this potential order and asked. "Gentlemen, tell me what should we do? Should we regret or do you think we can take the challenge?". The team understood the importance of this order. Moreover, when they were asked to make the decision, they felt ownership in the decision-making and the consequent benefits to the company. They accepted the challenge. Having accepted, the team worked hard and fulfilled the order on time. We not only delivered these 10 nos on time but continued to get further orders and ended up supplying over 100 nos. This type of taking joint decision grew in the company and resulted in gaining more customers in the process.

I realized the difference between owning a job and just doing a job and the phenomenal difference it can bring.

CHAPTER FORTY-NINE

Hornet's Nest

Decision-making is one of the most important activities in our professional and personal life. Not taking a decision is also a decision. However, it should be based on the analysis of the situation. Sometimes we feel comfortable not taking any action since we "feel' that the current situation is fine. We fear that if we analyze the situation, we may be required to take some tough decisions that may be painful to execute (why stir the hornet's nest).

I remember an incident, 2 decades back. I was explaining to an overseas customer about our company. One of the points we mention was that our company has not lost a single day of production on account of a labour strike. The customer immediately responded, "Maybe one of the parties is weak and not ready for a tough and fair bargain, fearing repercussion". I am not competent to comment on whether the management or the labour union was weak or strong. But this comment from a customer made me realise that if things are looking fine, it does not necessarily mean that everything is fine. We need to do a reality check to ascertain ....

1. Whether we are really in a good situation

Some of my friends don't go for health check-ups, since there are no symptoms. But only after you go through the health check-up you can say whether there is anything wrong or not. Likewise, we should analyse the current situation and then only conclude that things are normal/ good.

2. Whether there are any potential risks in the long run

Let us say, for example, our products are well-accepted in the market. Whether to keep the status quo or introduce another product to ensure business continuity is a choice the company should take, based on due diligence of the situation. Status-quo is an easier option as it is not going to impact in the short term. It may have a ramification in the longer run. There are several examples of failures on account of the status quo. Black burry phones were ruling the "business people mobile" market. They were sticking to their products and finally failed.

You may remember Toyota's Qualis. It was a very successful product in the Indian market. However, Toyota decided to stop it and introduced Innova. It may not have been an easy decision to stop a successful product and introduce a new product at a higher price. However, it was a big success.

3. Whether we are compromising on the latent potential of the situation.

You as a team leader may not be telling your team member that they need to improve. Because you feel that it would displease him or her. Hence you maintain the status quo thus compromising the latent potential of the team.

Likewise, in our personal life too, we need to question our status quo to see whether there is something that we need to do to improve our lives. Our relationship with the spouse and children may look superficially nice. But it may be because each one has given up on improving the relationship. Please review the same. At times stirring the hornet's nest is essential.

CHAPTER FIFTY

CONTENT & CONSISTENCY

In the year 2021, I started writing and posting a blog a week. When I started writing, I had 2 challenges. One is the content and the other is the consistency. I was wondering whether I would find enough topics to share. Also, whether I would be in a position to do it consistently.

It is often said that when you dig a well, you get water to the extent you dig. Likewise, the more and more you dig into your experience you will get more and more ideas to share. After I sowed the thought of writing the blogs in my mind, the subconscious mind worked on it regularly and kept throwing ideas. (You may like to read my 32nd chapter "The law of attraction" wherein I mentioned, "The unconscious mind is highly powerful and if we can sink some of our thoughts into this unconscious mind, it works for you even without you knowing of it".)

The challenge of *consistency* was more difficult. As I was a working professional, I wrote blogs on the weekend. Writing a blog takes not less than 4 hours. Like anyone else I also face the inertia (lethargy) to sit down and write. I overcame the inertia by using a catalyst.

After I posted the first few blogs, it became an implicit commitment to my readers that I would be posting the blogs every week. I used to receive responses from many, sharing their views on my blog, which encouraged and worked as a catalyst. Some of the readers sent me reminders on Saturday when the blog did not reach them by 7 AM. This kept me motivated. I find this system of making a public commitment works a lot to overcome any lethargy. I covered this concept extensively in my book *French Fries*, in the chapter “The Second Law of Motion”.

I am sharing the above to drive a point that the application of our learning is very important. As you may observe, I have used 2 of the tips that I shared in this book.

Kindly excuse me if the above sounds like blowing my trumpet. The objective of my writing is to convey, “If I can do it, you can do it as well. You may be already doing something that you love (apart from your profession). If not, I urge you to explore. It is fascinating to create something that you have been desirous of doing. It gives immense satisfaction.

CHAPTER FIFTY-ONE

WILLPOWER – SKILL OR MUSCLE OR HABIT

Willpower is something that I always wondered about. Sometimes, I exercise my willpower to control my anger and behave decently (!!!), and at a different point in time, in a similar situation, I lose my temper.

In this context, I would like to share with you what I learnt about "Willpower" in "The Power of Habit" by Charles Duhigg.

Starbucks and the likes have a big issue in handling customers. They focus on providing an excellent customer experience in their store. Every customer is different. Some of them may behave rudely. Some may be in a hurry requiring a quick service. The person on the counter needs to handle each of them with a smile and deliver the experience which is expected out of Starbucks. As mentioned in the words of Howard Behar, the former President of Starbucks, "We're not in the coffee business serving people but we are in the people business serving coffee. Our entire business model is based on fantastic customer service without that we are toast". ("we are toast" means we are ruined).

Initially, the researchers believed that willpower is a skill and once it is learnt then people can use it whenever such a situation occurs. But it was found that people are not able to consistently use it every time. If it is a skill, like swimming or driving, it should be possible to use it every time. This led them to think about whether Willpower is like a muscle. In the case of a muscle, by practicing weight lifting, we can strengthen the muscles and handle heavier weights for a longer time. To ascertain whether Willpower is like a muscle, the researchers selected a set of people and gave them the training to practice willpower by making them sign up for Gyms (for the people who never exercise). These exercises certainly helped them to build discipline in their life and helped them to handle situations better, but they did not assure employees to avoid anger at the point of sale.

After several such research, Starbucks came up with a structured program. When a newcomer joins, he was given a manual. Amongst other things, the manual contained a blank page with a heading, "When a customer is unhappy I plan to ......". The employee was asked to think of all possible unpleasant situations and asked to write down how they would react to such situations. After that, the managers would make a role play to help the employees to practice the behavior. By practicing it, again and again, it became a habit.

Coming back to where I started, i.e. controlling ourselves to handle anger, we can envision the situations that could test our willpower. Write down how you want to behave in such situations. If possible, roleplay it with your friends, if not, roleplay it in your mind. This would help you to build your willpower and make such behaviors a habit.

CHAPTER FIFTY-TWO

THOUGHTS

சிந்தனைகள் அற்ப காலமே
ஜீவிக்கின்றவை. அவை
காலாவதி ஆவதற்குள்
அவற்றுக்கு செயல்வடிவம்
கொடுத்து விடுங்கள்.

Thoughts survive for a very short duration. Before it expires, transform them into action.

Thoughts are generated continuously in our minds. For most of us, it is an uncontrolled action. There are a few people who can control their thoughts, maybe through meditation or some yogic practices. I am not going to talk about all these. Not my cup of tea.

The small chit of paper, shown in the above image, was found on my father's table under the glass. I had never noticed it when he was alive. He was born in 1929 and accomplished quite many things in his life period. I have huge respect for his achievement, like most of you for your parents.

I am not sure whether he wrote this sentence, or he noted this from somewhere else. Whatever it may be, I found it to be very profound.

Every minute, rather every second we are bounced with several thoughts in our minds. Some of them are meaningful and useful, and others not. I am a strong believer in the functioning of our subconscious mind. When we desire something strongly, our subconscious mind throws several thoughts at us. Most of us relish it for a moment and move on. That thought dies down and the next one emerges. Successful people generally convert these ideas into actions. The handwritten note in the above picture mentions just that.

It is needless to mention that every thought need not be converted to action. When a useful thought emerges, I note it down on my mobile or diary, or laptop. It helps me review it at a later point in time and decide what to do with it. If we find something worth the while, we should initiate the action immediately.

For eg. A person working on a shop floor may get thoughts regarding how to improve productivity. These thoughts may strike the person when he is traveling to work or having a bath or eating or attending some other meeting. Please note it down immediately, if not possible, at the next possible occasion. Evaluate them at leisure and execute.

You may get an idea about how to surprise your spouse on a birthday, probably the birthday is 10 months away. Please note it down on your mobile.

As a student, if you get a thought of skilling yourself in some area, please initiate action in that direction before the thought expires.

While I am attending a meeting, I get thoughts on how I can apply what I hear in the meeting to some other area. I immediately note it down. If I don't note it, I am sure to forget. If I force myself to remember, I can not concentrate on the meeting. Noting it down helps me not to forget and to focus on the meeting.

I noticed a good practice by my Japanese colleagues. When someone makes a presentation, they do not interrupt the presentation, even if it goes on for 1 hour. I could see them making notes. At the end of the presentation, they will ask questions referring to the slide number. This helps the presenter to make the presentation without any disturbance. Moreover, some of the questions that come to our mind in an earlier slide may get answered in the later slides. They do not keep their questions in their mind to ask.

Thoughts survive for a very short duration. Before it expires, transform them into action.

CHAPTER FIFTY-THREE

SUBORDINATING FEELINGS TO PURPOSE

"Subordinating feelings to the purpose" is one of the most powerful statements that I have read. I think I read this in the famous book "The seven habits of highly effective people", maybe, 20 years ago.

When we embark on an important initiative or assignment, we may be faced with situations in which we may choose to do something that is easier or more interesting but may not lead us to the desired result.

A simple example could be seen during dieting. We will find it difficult to subordinate our feelings (desire for eating rich food) to our purpose of being on diet, though we know very well that rich food will add to our weight.

Similarly in a game like cricket, where both individual excellence and team excellence are celebrated, some of the yesteryear players, especially in the Test match format, were accused of playing to make their records and not playing for the team. They failed to subordinate their feelings to the purpose (winning the game). Hence the team (the country image) failed.

Very often similar situations can be encountered even in our working environment. Some of the departments and people may be working for individual efficiency and not for the company's effectiveness and efficiency. This may be because the department's efficiency can be very easily seen outside and hence gets better recognition. Here the company's purpose gets sub-ordinated.

As a student, when I was studying at Coimbatore Institute of Technology, a friend of mine called Vaidyanathan was studying at PSG College, Coimbatore. I meet him very often and he was a studious guy who was focusing on his studies. He always advised me to focus on my studies. I will come back to my hostel fully charged to study. The moment my friends invite me to join them to watch a movie, all my resolve to focus on my study will be subordinated to entertainment. Fortunately, it was under some control and I managed to come out of college with decent marks. Vaidyanathan went to the US and I heard that he was doing extremely well.

Many of us in our professional careers would be faced with the situation of upskilling ourselves through some courses, for which we need to sacrifice time and money. We may find it difficult to sacrifice time as our urge for enjoying life may overpower us. Unless we subordinate that feeling we can not achieve the purpose.

If you want to achieve something in life, learn to Subordinate your feelings to your Purpose.

CHAPTER FIFTY-FOUR

EIGHTY TWENTY

At dinner, my wife had prepared a rich and heavy dinner. As I finished dinner stomach full, she told me that there is also fruits for dinner. Unfortunately, my stomach was full, and I could not take more, though I understand that taking some fruit at dinner is good for my health.

This happens in many situations in our life. We spend most of our time with useless or mundane activities and finally, we are left with no time for doing something good for us. It is not uncommon to see us wasting time in front of the TV, binge-watching serials. Instead, the time could be better spent following our passion or upgrading our skills.

I have come across people who fill up their time with routine activities and thus do not have any time for improving themselves and contributing in a better way to the organization. It takes a little bit of an effort to analyze the activities that a person is doing and make modifications to ensure that they were able to do the activities in a much shorter time. I am sure you have heard, "The work expands to fill time". I believe that the converse is also true to a certain extent. If our day is packed with activities, we find ways and means of doing all that. I try to do it often, by filling the day with some improvement activities.

Sometimes I succeed and sometimes fail. But it is much better than not attempting to do anything.

When I started my career with HCL in Dehradun, in the mid-1980s, I was introduced to Mr. PK Dhawan and his family by my neighbor in Pondicherry. My neighbor's daughter Ms. Sunitha was married to Mr. Dhawan. He was running one of the biggest businesses in Dehradun at that time. He and his wife were kind enough to invite me to their house for dinner many times during my stay in Dehradun. We had several casual conversations. I admired the way he used to talk about his business and his employees. Mr. Dhawan told me that he always ensured that his managers were occupied only 80% of the time so that they have 20% of time left for improving themselves and the organization. In case the workload increases beyond 80%, he told me that he would get one more person or reallocate work to ensure that the employee was not occupied for more than 80% in the routine job. I found this to be quite helpful in my career and found many successful people follow this. Sometimes we may not have a boss who believes in this. In such a case, I feel it is still possible for us to use our creativity to reduce the time to do the routine job and create time for improvement activities.

It will be worthwhile to specifically allocate some time in your calendar for doing some work that will address your future and not the present. This could be studying future trends in your area of work or automating some of the mundane activities or trying out small improvements or improving your skill with Excel/ PowerPoint/ letter writing/ etc. Failing in any of these attempts is not shameful, but failing to make such attempts is shameful.

CHAPTER FIFTY-FIVE

PLUS ONE

Before joining Larsen & Toubro, I worked for a startup company called General Optics (Asia) Limited, Pondicherry. They were manufacturing optical systems. I worked under a boss called Ramaswamy. He did his management studies at XLRI. He was a very simple person and had no complicated attitude. He was easy to approach, and I learnt a lot from him. He often said, "Arul, if you want to grow in your career you have to be *Plus One* than others", meaning, you need to run an extra mile compared to others around you if you want to grow. I could see people with such attitudes grow in their careers.

During your long career, you will be working in various departments and probably different companies. The caliber of the people you work with will be different in different companies. Please note that irrespective of how good you are, what matters is how good are you in comparison with the people around you, i.e. in comparative terms you need to perform better than them.

You need to show that you can do *Plus One* compared to others.

You can show "Plus One" capabilities with technical solutions or with interpersonal solutions. Understanding and delivering what your customers (internal or external) require makes you the most sought-after person in your department. It increases your visibility and enhances the image of your department with others. Tell me, which boss does not like a person who can increase the department's stature with internal or external customers?

I started my career with a company called Hindustan Reprographics Limited (later called HCL Limited) in Dehradun, situated in northern India. I joined as a graduate engineer trainee in their machine shop and toolroom. Michael Martyr joined this company as an Asst Supervisor for the machine shop. He was very good at his job. He was still better in terms of talking to people and making friends irrespective of the hierarchy. He was an honest and straightforward person. Both of us were bachelors at that time and we got along very well and spent the weekends exploring the nearby places. He used to help everyone on the shop floor and assumed the responsibility of the full shop whenever his senior was not present. He listened to the requirements of internal customers and satisfied their needs. This attitude of his was noticed by the management and he was promoted earlier than others. Michael later grew to much higher levels and became Senior General Manager of a mid-sized hydraulic component manufacturing company. After this, he worked as an Executive Director of a private limited company in the field of industrial cutting blades. This was possible because he exhibited *Plus One* capability compared to his colleagues.

The *Plus One* concept helped me and many others to grow in the organization, so why not for you?

CHAPTER FIFTY-SIX

COMMUNICATION

It is very common to witness the following communication between a team leader (TL) and his team member (TM).

TL: Has the proposal reached the client?

TM: I sent it yesterday.

TL: When will the assembly line restart?

TM: We're waiting for spare parts.

TL: At what time is the meeting with the client?

TM: We need to leave our office at 2:00 PM.

Though the above responses seem to be appropriate, on a second look you will understand that they are short of something and is not a complete answer to the question. Probably the following could be a more appropriate response.

TM: I do not know whether it has reached the client, but I sent it yesterday. I will check now.

TM: The assembly line is expected to start by around 8 PM. We are waiting for the receipt of spare parts by 6 PM.

TM: The meeting is at 3:00 PM for which we may have to start at 2:00 PM from our office.

Another set of conversations could be as follows

TL: When will you complete the proposal to the customer?

TM: We are verifying the specification.

TL: I asked when you will complete the proposal to the customer.

TM: There are some new items in the specification which we are checking with the engineering.

TL: Still you are not answering my question. When will you complete the proposal to the customer?

TM: After we get the response from Engineering, we will complete the proposal.

Such communications go on and on. Slowly it becomes clear that the person is not having an idea about when he can make the proposal. Maybe he's waiting for some confirmation from another department. In such a case the answer could be, "I'm not able to estimate, as I don't have a commitment from the engineering department regarding the new requirement in this specification".

On many occasions, we find people not providing direct answers to the questions that are being asked. For career growth, clear communication is one of the important traits one needs to learn and practice.

At this juncture, I would like to cite the famous reference in Ramayana written by Kambar (In Tamil). When Hanuman returns from Sri Lanka, where he went in search of Sita, at the behest of Rama, he mentions to Rama "கண்டனென், கற்பினுக்கு அணியை, கண்களால்". This means, "found her, the one who is a symbol of chastity, with my eyes".

Hanuman knows that Rama is waiting anxiously to know whether Hanuman met Sita in Sri Lanka and whether she is fine. So, he communicates using a short sentence but communicates that 1. He found her 2. She is chaste and 3. He saw her with his eyes. This is cited as one of the best examples of communication.

You may be extremely good at your work but if you have difficulty communicating to the point it may hamper your progress.

CHAPTER FIFTY-SEVEN

Association Matters

"Tell me about your friend I will tell who you are" is an adage. The people with whom we associate have a large bearing on our personal and professional growth.

Before I proceed further, I would like to differentiate friendship and association. I can recall my college days wherein there were a group of people who had an aspiration of going to the US for their higher studies. They used to hang around together. I know that some of them do not like each other, in fact, they hate each other. Nonetheless, they stayed together. They were associating with each other to achieve their goal, despite their differences.

On the other hand, a friend is someone who cares about your growth, whether or not he is in a position to help you in your growth. He is the one who knows about you a bit more than what you know about yourself. He is the one who becomes happier than you when you achieve something. Haven't you experienced this, your friend telling others about your achievement more than you tell others?

If you are lucky, you may have friends with a similar urge for achievement. If not, do not worry, you can identify friends with similar interests. I do understand that friendships are not created based on some ulterior motive. However, if the motive is good, I think, there is no harm in identifying people with common interests and making friends with them.

Alternatively, you can associate with people having a similar drive for achievement so that it keeps your fire on. Being a member of some forums or participating in various competitions helps you a lot to associate yourself with such people.

You might have heard the phrase "Attitude determines your Altitude". Likewise, I would like to say that "Association augments Achievement".

I worked at Larsen & Toubro for 3 decades. The structure of the company by itself provides this association. People of similar professional levels from various units in India and abroad are required to meet quite often in the training programs & assessment centers. This helps to associate with people of similar drive and aspiration. When you are amongst the people with drive, you also get infected with it automatically.

If you are chasing a goal or want to achieve a certain position in your professional life, I sincerely recommend that you associate with people who also have the thrust to reach certain heights. It does not matter whether they are chasing the same dream or something different.

PS: Please do not misunderstand that association with like-minded people is essential for success. According to me, it greatly assists in achieving our goal faster. Several extraordinary people have succeeded despite the fact the whole world discouraged them.

CHAPTER FIFTY-EIGHT

ARE YOU DISSATISFIED? THAT'S GREAT !!!

Dissatisfaction is the seed of creativity. Many revolutionary inventions are caused due to the dissatisfaction of the inventor with the current situation.

While the companies work toward introducing products to satisfy customer needs, such creative thoughts are born out of employees who are dissatisfied with the status quo. This dissatisfaction drives them to bring out new products. The demand for better products may not come from the customer. In many cases, the customer does not know what he needs. Inventors and entrepreneurs identify the potential needs of people and create a product to meet those unsaid requirements. All these emanate from dissatisfaction with something.

Hence dissatisfaction is a very important tool that could help you to grow and to contribute to the organization.

There are situations where a person likes his job responsibility but is upset with the way it is being executed.

This dissatisfaction if channeled properly can lead to identifying better methods of doing things.

You may be dissatisfied with your current role as it may not be aligned with your aspiration. When this dissatisfaction increases, people look for alternative routes to fulfill their aspirations. This could be changing jobs, improving their skill set, taking up higher education, changing departments, taking up challenging assignments, etc.

However, each one has a certain break-even point for withstanding the dissatisfaction. Some people have a very high tolerance and consequently have a very high break-even point, which prevents them from improving.

I have seen some of my younger colleagues at 35 and 40 years spending lakhs of rupees in doing MBA and launching their careers to a higher orbit. This stems from their dissatisfaction with the current role which is not meeting their aspiration.

Sometimes people quit their job and start businesses in the middle of their careers to follow their passion such as becoming an entrepreneur or doing social service, etc.

Do not explore new avenues without analysing your current status properly. Please understand that the existing role itself may provide ample opportunity for improvement. If you focus on possible improvements in that area, it can help you achieve growth and satisfaction. Please identify the areas that create dissatisfaction for you. I will not hesitate to suggest that you should nurture dissatisfaction to such a level that it gives you the necessary thrust to act. However, dissatisfaction, if not channelized properly, can lead to frustration and depression. Please tread cautiously here.

The feeling of satisfaction inhibits improvement and growth. Often, I find people who do not improve are the ones who feel satisfied with their performance.

Cultivate positive dissatisfaction and leverage it for your growth.

CHAPTER FIFTY-NINE

IF YOU HAVEN'T MADE A MISTAKE, MOST LIKELY YOU HAVE NOT TRIED ANYTHING NEW

I know the title is too long, however, I kept it to convey the central meaning of the chapter. By the way, the long titles are not uncommon, just to cite one which I came across recently for a Netflix web series is "The Woman in the House Across the Street from the Girl in the Window". Please do not ask me what it means.

We will come across colleagues who claim that they have not met with any failures, while we may have failed many times.

During the early 1990s ISO certification was becoming very important to companies especially if they are exporting their products. The company where I was working at that time embarked on getting certified under

ISO. They conducted training programs for all its employees and a consultant was hired. The first mock audit was conducted, and all the functional areas were audited strictly, and the result was presented to the Chief Executive. Almost all the functional areas had several NCs (Non-Conformities, which means failure to adhere to the system) except 1 department which had only 1 NC (Non-Conformity). We were wondering how that department managed to get only 1 NC. When the consultant presented the details of the NCs, we understood that the only NC that they got was "No system is available for audit". He did not even try to establish the ISO system hence he made only one mistake where as others made many.

TATA Motor's venture into car manufacturing is a classic case study. Competing with global players in a price-sensitive car market is not a joke. TATA introduced Nano but it was a big failure. Many other cars introduced were also failures. But the cars & SUVs introduced recently are having great success. I am sure the various failures have taught them lessons that made them very successful now.

In my career, I have made many decisions some of which failed and some succeeded. So will be the case with many others as well.

I was probably one of the persons instrumental in introducing automation to the tire industry. Though we executed the first automation project in India for a tyre company, we (as a company) failed to capitalize on the early mover advantage we had, due to a wrong approach to this new business. Learning from this mistake, I changed my way of working for promoting new products. The company fine-tuned its approach to new business and successfully introduced many new products.

We normally see only the success of people, there are several failures behind that success which does not come surface. As they say, Edison made 9999 attempts that failed before he invented the light bulb.

Never shy to try out new things in your personal or professional life as long as it is within ethical boundaries and is in the right direction. Please ensure that you take the necessary precautions.

CHAPTER SIXTY

RESPONDING TO FAILURES

You are judged more by your reaction to failure than by failure itself since failure is part and parcel of anyone's growth story.

In my previous role as a marketing person, we had secured a large order to supply over 100 machines to a customer in Europe. During the execution of this order, we faced difficulties in terms of meeting the delivery commitments. The project timeline was suffering and the Project Head called me for a discussion at their site in Europe. He told me, "Arul, we are dealing with your company for many years. We have come across similar issues in the past with your company and other major suppliers. What is important is how you respond to problems and provide the remedy to the customer. In this current order execution, we find it is missing. Please discuss this with your management and find a quick solution."

It was a very good piece of advice for me.

Even in our personal lives, we may come across failures/ challenges. How we handle such challenges defines our character and worth. There will be situations when we did not get promoted though we feel that we deserve it. Some people reduce their commitment to work and a few others work harder and smarter so that they make themselves more eligible for the promotion.

A student may miss getting admission to a premier institute. I have seen quite a few students who skip a year and again try and make it up to their preferred college and branch of study.

I remember a story that was part of my 10th standard English syllabus. It was called "The Verger". It was about a verger (attendant in a church) of St. Peter's Church at Neville Square in London. His job was to ring the giant bell in the church whenever it was required. One day the Church management decided that all its employees including the attendant should be literate. Unfortunately, the verger was not educated and hence he lost his job. While he was roaming on the road, he wanted to smoke and finds that there are no petty shops selling cigarettes. With the small money that he had, he starts a shop. The story goes on to mention that he opened several shops and became a rich man. He visited the bank every week and deposited the money collected from the shops. Since he was an important customer of the bank, the manager received him every time and did all the paperwork himself. One day, the bank manager was replaced with a new manager. The (ex) verger visited the bank to deposit the money. As per the practice, he went to the manager's room and found a new man, and introduced himself to him. He handed over the money for the deposit. The Manager filled out the challan and asked him to sign. The verger said, that he did not know to read and write and he put his thumb impression. The manager was astonished and asked him,

"Without knowing to read and write if you could be so rich, what if you had known to read and write". The verger replied, "I would be ringing the bell as the verger of St Peter's church".

Failures are moments to prove our resolve and commitment to the objectives. Sometimes they throw open completely a new avenue for us to explore and explode (in a positive manner).

CHAPTER SIXTY-ONE

INVISIBLE

"Do your duty and do not expect the rewards", is one of many learnings from the Bhagavad Gita. (my knowledge of Gita is next only to Zero. This is just hearsay from elders).

Some people follow this literally. They do a wonderful job, but they do not let others know about it. Not because of any secrecy, but because that is their character. I consider them to be invisible to the management's eyes.

Though during annual appraisals (evaluation of performance) the management is expected to evaluate the performance of the employees based on their achievements, it is not a secret that the opinion created by the juniors throughout the year weighs very much in the annual ratings. This opinion is created from various actions done by the person during the year. If a person shares his achievements with his superior periodically, the superior can relate them to the list of achievements mentioned in his appraisal sheet during the annual evaluation.

For eg., let's assume the annual target for a salesperson is Rs. 100 cr. Despite his best efforts, he could sell only Rs. 80 cr. When he presents this to his superior, the superior will most certainly consider this as a poor performance and rate the salesperson poor (just a crude example). In reality, maybe, one of the biggest customers went out of business, and in that circumstance getting an order for Rs. 80 Cr itself was a very big achievement. Probably the salesperson had put extraordinary efforts to get increased orders from other customers. If this was not expressed by the junior during the course of the year, it might not be convincing at the end of the year.

The engineers who work on reducing the cycle time of a process and if they regularly update the improvements it becomes easy at the end of the year.

The above examples are quantitative and hence easy for people to see. But several functions have qualitative objectives. For eg., HR will have difficulty quantifying many of their initiatives like training, culture, welfare, etc. Updating regularly helps a lot in making yourself visible to your team leader or management.

We also have people who overdo this action by reporting small improvements or exaggerating small things. It could work for some time. Later, it will backfire.

Once, I was explaining the above to a junior colleague and told him that he should inform me about the good work he was doing regularly. He asked me a question, "Is it not your responsibility to find out what I am doing". I was taken aback. In a lighter vein, it was like the sudden realization by the hero in the movie "Vedham Puthithu" (sorry for referring to an old Tamil movie) when a small boy makes the hero realize about hero's presumption. The director depicted it, as someone slapping the hero. It was my "Vedham Puthithu" moment. If interested, you may watch the clip with English subtitles, by searching on youtube for "Vedham puthithu best scenes".

From that moment I made it a point to identify silent performers too. So, my advice to the seniors is to identify whether you have silent performers and take care of them. On the other hand, for the people who are being evaluated, my advice is, please make yourself visible and make the job of evaluation easier for your seniors.

CHAPTER SIXTY-TWO

HABITS & REWARDS

One of the most difficult activities for a human being is to form a good habit and to get rid of the bad (or not so-desired) habits. Since almost everyone is suffering (!) from this issue, no wonder there are several research and theories on this.

For eg., forming a simple and good habit like a morning walk can be achieved by joining another friend who is regular in this. It gives the additional benefit of chatting with a friend while going for walking. Normally human beings do a job when they get rewarded for the same. In this case, the opportunity to share thoughts with a friend is a great reward that motivates the habit of a morning walk.

I published blogs every week for more than 1 year without a break. This was possible because I received positive comments from my readers. In case there was no response from anyone then, probably, I would have stopped it within a few weeks.

Getting rid of a "not so desired" act is not that easy as we receive some reward for doing that activity.

Charles Duhigg in his book "The Power of Habit" explains this with the Habit Loop.

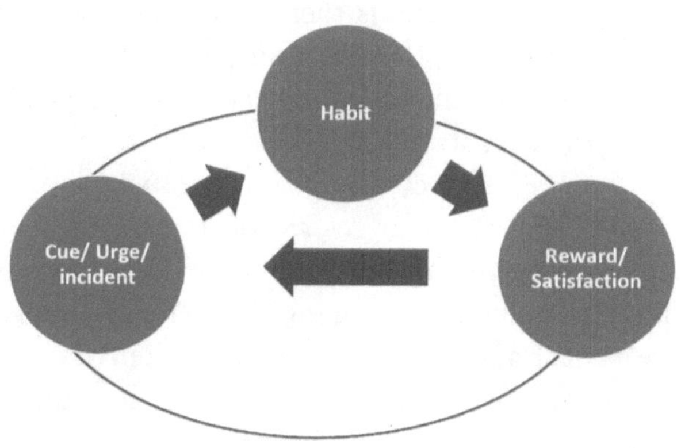

Habit Loop

These habits can be as simple as nail biting or snacking or as serious as smoking or being an alcoholic. Everything follows the same cycle. A cue or urge or a situation makes the person carry out their habit. Once they act, they get a reward which may be happiness or satisfaction.

For example, a person may smoke only when he is on a business tour. In this case, the tour environment (maybe loneliness/ companionship/ business meeting) is the cue that makes him take on smoking. At the end of smoking, he may get a sort of satisfaction (overcoming loneliness or a feeling of friendship). For some people, when they feel nervous, they bite their nails and this action engages them for a while and probably gives them some comfort in that situation.

If we want to change a habit that we do not desire to pursue, we should identify what is the cue and what is the reward/satisfaction we get out of this action. Once we understand what the cue is then we can do one of the 2 things. 1. Ensure that the situation does not arise 2. If it arises can you do some other activity by which we get the same reward or satisfaction?

For example, if a person takes alcohol whenever he is alone and if he wants to get rid of it then, he may try to avoid the situation of being alone by doing some other activity like going to the gym or a friend's house or relative's house and spend the time in a better way?

I know it is easier said than done. I am sure the above knowledge will help you to change at least a few of the habits that you don't desire to have. But the challenge lies in identifying the cues and rewards.

Wish you all the best.

CHAPTER SIXTY-THREE

YOUR TIME

I strongly believe in "the Right Person, at the Right Place, and at the Right Time".

Our success is linked to these 3 principles.

The culmination of these 3 things brings success to the person or the business.

It is not enough if one or two out of the 3 are present. Identifying all the 3 is not that easy. If it was, success may not be elusive to many.

As you know, a company recruits a person based on the people who attend the interview. You may increase the number of people by searching more on job portals, but you cannot rule out that there may be better people outside. Even in the beauty contest, the beauty queen is the person who is the most beautiful among the participants. Am sure there will be a more beautiful person who has not participated, (the right person but not at the right place).

Everyone desires to be the Right Person, at the Right Place, and at the Right Time. While we can at best make ourselves the right person at the right place, the right time may elude us or may never come. If I remember right, Maxworth, a company that started selling vegetables as a corporate business 20 years ago through air-conditioned stores, faced an ill fate. But 10 years later many such stores opened up. Maxworth had the right product and the right market, but the Time was not right (too early).

You may be the most eligible person to become the CEO or Country head, but that position should become vacant for it to be given to you. When will it happen? It may happen by design, i.e the incumbent may retire in the next couple of years. Or, it may happen by chance, i.e. the incumbent may resign for some reason / sent out for some reason and hence the post falls vacant. Or. It may never happen, your ill luck.

PV Narashima Rao became the PM since Rajiv Gandhi was assassinated. When the right time came (though accidentally) he became the PM, because he was the right person at the right place.

If you recall Tamil Nadu politics during the first DMK rule in 1967, the Chief Minister CM Annadurai passed away, the senior most Minister was VR Nedunchzhiyan. He was at the right place and the time was right for him to take the CM post. But Karunanidhi took over as the CM since he was the right person (could get the support of all) at that place (though not at the same seniority)

Out of the three, the Person, the Place, and the Time, the right time comes to some people when they do not expect it.

If you have not got your break, please wait, your time has not arrived. The time will come. It is not in our hands. In the meanwhile, you may increase the probability by making yourself fit for the position and being at the place where you may be needed.

Wish you all the best.

CHAPTER SIXTY-FOUR

COMPLIMENTS

One of the biggest pitfalls for a person is falling for praise.

Almost everyone likes to be praised. (maybe, except for Mr. AR Rahman – his facial expressions do not change even a bit when he is being praised. It will look as though he is listening to a boring college lecture). At least, I can say, most people (including me) enjoy when being praised. I guess there is nothing to be ashamed of. At the same time, we need to be conscious about, whether to believe in it or not. A self-aware person will know what he is worth and what he is not. Even when a person praises him, he will understand whether it is genuine, or it is being done to impress him.

When a person grows in his profession/career this becomes a big problem. People associated with him praise him which may not be genuine. When that person thinks it is true and acts as though it is true, then his downfall starts. A self-aware person may enjoy the praise but knows it need not be true.

We have seen this many times in politics. Many people who were famous in other fields, like celluloid were made to believe by their followers that they can make it up big in politics. But only a very few people succeed.

In the case of Hitler, their generals kept on saying that Hitler was great and that all his plans were working out well. Hitler believed it and led Germany & the world to a disaster.

When someone praises you and if there is a truth in it, please acknowledge their compliment but do not let it go into your head.

If someone praises you and you know it is not true, it is better to tell him/ her that you do not like such false praises. At least they will know that you do not welcome such false compliments. Such a polite and firm response from you will avoid such unrealistic appreciations, which is a potential pitfall.

CHAPTER SIXTY-FIVE

QUALITY

When I started my professional career, I was told that for a company to succeed it should focus on three core areas Quality, Cost, and Delivery. It tacitly implied that if one parameter is lower it can be adjusted by changing the other 2 parameters, meaning, if the quality is lower we can reduce the selling price and still sell the product. I think the scenario has changed. Today, Quality cannot be grouped with Cost and Delivery. Because you can't negotiate on quality whereas you can, on cost and delivery.

In most of the engineered products (such as automobiles, machinery, and white goods), customers are not ready to accept lower quality. Quality is the foundation without which we cannot build a business.

According to me, quality for a business is like breathing for a human. There can be no priority that can be fixed for breathing over other activities that we perform. You may be doing many things like exercise, walking, yoga, and dieting for maintaining the body in a fit condition. All these cannot compete with breathing. There is no necessity to tell how important breathing is. If breathing stops everything stops.

Breathing is done at a subconscious level. We are not putting any conscious effort to control our breathing. Even quality should be like this. The company's routine processes should churn out quality products, at a subconscious level.

In today's environment irrespective of whether you can give a better cost or delivery, people are not ready to look at lower-quality products. For example, today if somebody offers a Fiat car or Ambassador car at a price that is more competitive and an ex-stock delivery compared to any of the cars available today, will anyone take it? Nobody will be ready to take this offer, because the expectation of people has changed.

We had several Chinese products that invaded our market like 2-wheelers, 4-wheelers, tires, machinery, and white goods. Where are they now? Most of them have faded out. The ones that stay in the market are the ones that are good in quality.

I feel Quality is not a function or a department, it is the personality or character of a company. It is to be felt by the customer and not something proved by the inspection report and quality audit.

Customer expectation of Quality in India has undergone a complete change in the past few decades. Every company and every person should realise it to be successful.

CHAPTER SIXTY-SIX

JOHARI WINDOW

Johari Window

I was taking a training session for a few youngsters, in which I referred to this Johari window. To my surprise, many of them were not aware of this. I consider the knowledge of the Johari window to be essential for every individual. Hence, I decided to add a chapter on it.

The Johari window was developed by 2 psychologists, Joseph Luft, and Harrington Ingham, in the year 1955. They named the model by combining their first names.

If you are already familiar with this concept you may skip reading this chapter or read it to refresh your memory.

This is a very interesting tool. The knowledge of this will help us to understand ourselves very well.

As per this concept, every individual has got 4 quadrants made on 2 axes. One axis represents what we know about ourselves and the other is the knowledge of others about us. (See figure above)

Open Self: This quadrant represents your character and capabilities that are known to you and also to others. For eg. If a person expresses his emotions (say love or anger) all the time and he is aware of it, people around him understand that he is a caring person, or he is an angry person. The person is also aware of it.

Blind Self: This quadrant represents your character and capabilities that you are not aware of, but others know about them.

For eg. If a person has the habit of hurting everyone and he is not aware of it, people around him know that he is a person who cares little for others' feelings, but the person may not be aware of it. You might have come across a situation where someone tells you about your behavior but you may feel it is not your personality. Please introspect whether this facet of your personality is in the blind spot that you are not aware of.

Hidden self: This quadrant represents your character and capabilities that are known to you but not known to others. Maybe because you do not explicitly exhibit such character and capabilities. Probably it is your secret area.

This quite often happens in many families. Many of us fail to express our care and love for our family members though we may have it in our hearts. Unless this is expressed it is impossible for someone to open our hearts to see it.

Unknown Self: this quadrant represents your character and capabilities that are not known to you and others.

These are normally the feelings that may be embedded at our subconscious level, of which we are not aware. However, these feelings have an impact on our actions. When such things are not noticeable by others, they fall into this category

In the above diagram, the four quadrants are shown in equal size. However, the size of each quadrant will vary to the extent that you are self-aware. For someone less aware of himself or herself, the area under "known to self" will be much smaller compared to the area under "not known to self".

For a person who is more self-aware of his or her character and capabilities, the area under "known to self" will be larger compared to the area under "not known to self".

Please work towards increasing the size of the area under "known to self" so that you know more about yourself and could leverage your strengths and mitigate your weaknesses.

CHAPTER SIXTY-SEVEN

CHECK BOX

During my initial years of married life, my wife accused me of Check Box ticking. I did not understand what she meant. It took some time.

Every couple wants to lead a happy married life. As we all know it needs some effort. It does not happen by itself. Efforts include spending time with each other, understanding each other, sharing experiences, appreciating one another's challenges, etc. When you drill down this further, it may result in some of the following actions: going out for dinner, listening to each other, sharing gifts on important occasions, etc. All these can be done with or without full involvement. When it is done without involvement, just to satisfy a list of actions, it is called "ticking the check box".

Let us take for an instant that a person comes home in the evening to spend quality time with his/ her spouse. Instead of spending time with the spouse, if he/ she is spending time watching web series or browsing the web, or talking to someone else on phone, he/ she is ticking the check box. But he/ she may feel, that he/ she has spent the evening with their spouse.

It is not only in our personal life. It is also applicable to our professional life.

In the engineering industry, it is quite normal to have a checklist to inspect a Machine or a component. The person in charge of the inspection will carry this check sheet and tick-mark various parameters as he inspects. This is a very effective method to ensure compliance with specifications.

However, when you consider activities that are not so technical but are more soft skill related like building trust or relationships, ticking the check box may not yield the result that you desire.

Functions like HR, Marketing, and Purchasing will fall under this category.

For example, in the marketing function, there is always pressure from the management that the marketing person should meet the customer quite often, say for example at least once a month. To satisfy this management requirement, the marketing person may visit the customer and tick the box. But what is more important is whether he has added value to the meeting or whether he has built a relationship.

Similarly, in the HR function, they may be providing training to the employees as per the stipulated norms like 5 days per year per employee (for eg). The box is ticked. But whether the employee got trained or not is not measured.

I am sure the above philosophy applies to all of us in our personal and professional life. A little more attention to this can improve our personal and professional life.

CHAPTER SIXTY-EIGHT

CHAMPION

When I started working with Japanese colleagues, I faced the following situation. Our team of Indian colleagues would share several instances of achieving something quite phenomenal. For eg. the completion of an assembly within three days whereas the normal lead time is six days, developing a component within three months whereas the normal lead time for development is six months, doubling sales in the last month of the financial year, i.e. March, etc. I used to find that such achievements never enthused my Japanese colleagues. I once asked one of my Japanese colleagues, "Are these not big achievements that need celebrations or at least acknowledgment?" He replied, "Arul san, we never take the champion data as an achievement. (Champion data means – once-in-a-while accomplishments) Because we may not be able to repeat it. Unless we can repeat such performances continuously, it is not going to be useful for the business. Hence anything that can be sustained continually only can be regarded as an achievement."

While such stand-alone achievements are required to meet certain specific challenges, they may not yield long-term benefits to the organization. Realizing this our team started working on structures that can support and sustain improvements. This attitude has certainly improved the performance of our unit. I am sure it will assist you in your personal and professional growth as well.

If you ask me whether such special accomplishments are required or not, I would say, yes, it is required. We (Indians) are good at it. We should not lose it. It will come in handy in times of emergency and special situations. But we should not get lost on its laurels.

CHAPTER SIXTY-NINE

THE MIRROR

"Change is the only thing that is constant in this world". I came across this phrase for the first time in early 1990. Later I found that it was a very old phrase. The Greek philosopher Heraclitus is credited with saying "The only constant in life is change".

Though we all believe in the above statement, the recent incidents strengthened our belief in this. The changes in technology and the geopolitical scenario that we are witnessing now are affecting everyone's personal and professional life like never before.

While we understand that change is the only constant thing, we fail to change ourselves continuously to stay relevant.

I get reminded of the speech by Steve Jobs to the graduating students at Standford University. He narrated 3 stories. The first one was about *connecting the dots*, the second one was about *love and loss and* the third one was about *death*. I would like to quote what he said as his third story. "When I was 17, I read a quote that went something like, if you live each day as if it was your last day, someday you'll most certainly be right. It made an impression on me, and since then, for the past 33 years, I looked in the mirror every morning and asked myself: if today were the last day of my life, would I want to do what I am about to do today? And Whenever the answer has been "No" for too many days in a row, I know I need to change something."

It is worth watching the speech of Steve Jobs again, even if you had already watched it. Easy to locate on Youtube. The 3rd story starts at the 9th minute.

Most of you would have watched this video as it has been circulating in social media for the past many years. We have an extended lesson to learn from this. If I stand in front of the mirror and ask myself "How long I have been doing this job in the manner that I am doing now?" And if the answer is, "may be too long". If this is the same answer that I get for many months, then there is something wrong. It means I am stagnating in whatever job I am doing. With the changes that are happening around us, it is merely impossible that we go about doing our job (personal or professional) in the same manner and believe that we are progressing.

Ask yourself the above question and examine the reply.

CHAPTER SEVENTY

REPUTATION

When we mention names like TATA, L&T, ITC, etc., it certainly relates to something like trust, quality, nation-building, caring for customers, etc. These are the values those brands have created in the minds of the people through their relentless focus on the virtues they hold close to their hearts. Whenever they come out with a product or service, we are sure that it would be a good one and we do not think twice before buying it.

When I visited the Passport Seva Kendra in Chennai, which is managed by TCS, the lady at the counter asked whether I would like to buy a leather cover for the passport. Normally when someone uses the opportunity to push their product, I refuse to take it. When the lady said it is from TATAs, I did not feel that they are pushing their product, though they are precisely doing the same. If it was some other company, I would have said NO. This is because of TATA's reputation as a company that respects people. I am sure most of you would share similar feelings.

It is not only true for companies. It is also true for individuals. How we behave creates an impression about us in the minds of others. When we talk to people, our image overshadows what we speak. In the book "7 Habits of Highly effective people", Steven Covey mentions this as "what you are shouts so loud that I do not hear what you say".

I was listening to a podcast, where they said "What people talk about you before you enter a room and after you leave the room is the reputation you have created".

This is very powerful. Yet people refuse to understand and work on it. If your reputation is to find fault and fight, no matter with what intention you approach the other person, it will end in a negative result. If your reputation is that of a solution seeker or provider, you will invariably end up with a solution.

In a professional career, this certainly helps in your growth. When your reputation is that of a problem solver, team player, a supporter of initiatives, etc., the management notices you and provides growth opportunities. If you are a person who normally looks at the negative side of all the initiatives, the management is most likely to ignore you.

About The Author

Arul Shanmugavelu is an engineer who furthered his education with a management degree. After working for a short period at HCL Limited and General Optics (Asia) Limited, he joined Larsen & Toubro Limited (L&T). In L&T, he worked for 30 years, in various functional areas such as purchase, import and export logistics, domestic & international marketing, customer service, and product development. During this period he traveled to many countries and dealt with people from various cultures. In 2014, he became the chief executive of one of the subsidiaries of L&T. At the time of publishing this book, he was heading Kobelco Industrial Machinery India Private Limited as its managing director.

Arul is passionate about sharing his knowledge with others. He conducts training programs on Effective Living, Fun with Finance, and Goal Setting. He is also actively involved in social service.

He lives in Chennai with his wife Sathya. Their daughter and son-in-law are practicing Doctors in Chennai and their son is doing his Doctorate in Robotics in the US.

His first book on career growth "French Fries" was well appreciated by the readers with a 5-star rating on Amazon.

He can be contacted at arulshanmugavelu@yahoo.com.

www.ingramcontent.com/pod-product-compliance
Lightning Source LLC
LaVergne TN
LVHW091317150826
845673LV00006B/1679

* 9 7 9 8 8 9 0 2 6 2 0 3 5 *